Paul Charles

The Pocket Essential

How To Succeed In The
Music Business

www.pocketessentials.com

First published in Great Britain 2002 by

Pocket Essentials, 18 Coleswood Road, Harpenden, Herts, AL5 1EQ

Distributed in the USA by Trafalgar Square Publishing,

PO Box 257, Howe Hill Road, North Pomfret, Vermont 05053

A CIP catalogue record for this book is available from the British Library.

ISBN 1-904048-06-4

2 4 6 8 10 9 7 5 3 1

Book typeset by Pdunk

Printed and bound by Cox & Wyman

Acknowledgements

Thanks to each and every one of the artists, managers and road crews who have worked with us and currently work with us at Asgard. To Paul Fenn for being the perfect partner to share these adventures with. To Christina Czarnik for keeping the wheels on the wagon and a copy of absolutely everything. To Ion Mills and Paul Duncan for the essential platform. To Andy and Cora without whom… and to Catherine for whom…

Contents

CONTENTS

1. How To Shine The Light

When man-about-town and publisher-in-chief Ion Mills took me out to lunch in Islington to discuss this book he asked me what an agent in the music business actually did. It's a popular and frequently asked question, "Yes I know you work in the music business but what do you actually do?" I suppose part of the assumption is that people in the music business actually do little or no work at all. I mean how could we when most of us (supposedly) don't get into our office until the crack of lunchtime? It's probably a more accurate complaint when directed at the last generation of agents who did tend to keep gentlemen's hours, but more about Tito later.

So you're an aspiring singer/songwriter or you've just had an idea to form a group with a bunch of your friends and you want and need to know what an agent can do for you and what else you're going to need to know to launch your career in this business they call show business. It's vitally important to ensure from the very start that you have your affairs in order. It's no use saying, "Oh this is fine for now. We'll sort it out later." Whether you are talking about The Beatles or Van Morrison or Chuck Berry or Sting – probably the majority of artists in fact – they've all made bad deals that they've ended up paying for throughout the remainder of their career. Now equally, you could probably say that if they had taken the time to get the perfect deal, well then maybe the chance, the golden opportunity, might have passed them by. That's certainly a distinct possibility and that doesn't mean that I'm suggesting you take whatever you can get. On the contrary, I'd have to say beware of anyone who tries to force you to sign a quick deal. There's always time to take a step back and weigh up your options and in this wee book of ours I'll endeavour to advise you exactly what those options are.

All you probably want to do is write songs and perform them on stage but you can't find a way to get started. From the outside the music business with all its apparent beautiful and cool people, buzzwords, in-phrases and jingo can appear quite daunting but the reality is that from the inside it's quite basic and very simple.

We'll discuss the various professionals you'll come into contact with and what exactly they should be doing for you. Why do you need a music publisher for instance when you've already got a record company? Do you really need a manager when you've already got a great lawyer? And then the big one, yes you know you need an agent and you've already got one, thank you very much, but why do you also need a promoter? We'll discuss where all your income will come from – providing of course you enjoy some degree of success. And then we'll try and show you where all your hard-earned cash will disappear to by showing you what kind of deals the various people involved in your career will offer you and what kind of commission you should expect to pay for the privilege of working with those representatives. We'll even make a few suggestions as to how to put your own personal dream team together.

The idea of this Pocket Essential is to present you with enough information so that you can make a start on the rocky roads of the music business either as an artist or on the business side. Along the way I'll let you in on a few short cuts, throw in a few tales and stories of some who have gone before you and, who knows, I might even get around to telling you how to make rain fall on stage on cue without electrocuting anyone and how to produce, not a white rabbit, but a beam of pure white light from inside a top hat.

2. The Big Picture

Before we go any further let's consider the big picture and how everyone fits into it.

The Artist.

The Manager.

The Agent – The Accountant – The Solicitor – The Tour Manager

The Publicist – The Radio Plugger

The Record Co. – The Publishing Co. – The Merchandising Co. – The Concert Promoter

The Record Producer – The Road Crew – The Additional Musicians

On top of this you have numerous other personnel: a stylist, a hairdresser, a dance instructor, a video director, a driver, an ambience director (drug dealer), a fitness instructor, a nanny, security, a business manager, a portfolio manager, a bank manager not to mention the odd hanger-on and old school friend or two.

I'm sure I've forgotten a few but undoubtedly they'll come knocking on your door before the end of the adverts.

Top of the pile (obviously) you have the artist and directly underneath the artist is the manager who's meant to liaise with all of those who act on behalf of the artist. All underneath that level are meant to report directly to the manager. For this template I'm dealing with how it should be, later on we can get into the numerous variations on the theme. I place the Agent, Accountant, Solicitor and Tour Manager on the next line only because they also act for, on behalf of and in the best interest of the artist. The four on the fourth tier (Record Co., Publishing Co., Merchandising Co. and Concert Promoter) primarily look after their own interests, and you'd expect them to because they are usually investing large sums of money. So your best interest isn't always necessarily going to be their best interest.

Let's talk about the manager. The manager should be a very creative person who can discover, invent and break an artist. It's vitally important that the manager share the artist's vision and passion. Let's consider a scenario set in the late 1970s. Punk music is giving the music scene its biggest and healthiest shake-up since Bill Hailey rattled his kiss curl. This geek walks in from the street into the offices of one of the prime punk labels. In the middle of all the bedlam and craziness the chap who runs the record company hears something in the geek's songs. He takes the geek under his wing, puts him in the recording studio with a hip producer and an extremely cool studio band, gives the geek an image of an aggressive wordsmith, puts together a powerhouse live band for the gigs and writes all the copy for the original adverts. The geek was Elvis Costello, the manager who invented him was Jake Riviera and both of them set off on a stormy and extremely successful 17-year relationship. Yes you can say Elvis had a talent, for he certainly had, and I'd also agree that you can't keep a great talent down, but I'd also have to say that the main difference between Elvis Costello and the Jags was Jake Riviera. So I suppose, what I'm saying, is that managers can and do make a difference. Other good examples would be Brian Epstein and The Beatles and Colonel Tom Parker and Elvis Presley.

I know it's very popular these days to claim that Brian Epstein negotiated a few bad deals on The Beatles' behalf. I'd have to disagree with that. He was ploughing pastures new; he was doing deals that had never been done before. Since then of course, those pioneering deals have been bettered. It's 40 years since, so we'd hope so wouldn't we? I mean it didn't really take long to develop the wheel once it had been invented. But without Brian Epstein I believe a lot of the artist power evident in the current music business wouldn't exist. Before Brian Epstein a lot of the managers were the stars. What the manager said was Gospel as far as the artists were concerned. Some took 50% of the income and some even paid the artist nothing but a weekly salary and still the majority of those artists said, yes sir, no sir and three bags full sir. To a great degree Mr Epstein changed all of that. Anyway don't get me started on The Beatles or this particular Pocket Essential may not fit into a suit full of pockets.

I'd say the single most important factor in choosing a manager is appointing someone who really cares about you and your music. Experience of the music business isn't really a necessity because your manager can be kept on the right tracks by your solicitor, accountant and agent. Don't go looking for the star manager. Don't think that just because he did it for Madonna, he'll do it for you. The music business graveyard is littered with artists who were star managers' pet projects. If you think about it, you're on a hiding to nothing if you take that route. The star manager can walk into his pet record company with any new band and win them a deal simply because of the number of units his main act is shifting. However, that's totally the wrong reason to be signed. If that's you or your group then I'm sure you'll find that when the record company start working on your project they are usually not committed to you in the way they need to be committed to you for you to have a chance at success. You are seen and tarnished as an indulgence and they'll traditionally do just enough to keep the star manager off their back.

So pick someone who totally believes in you. Don't feel you have to make a decision overnight. Hang out with your prospective manager, get to know them extremely well. Throw them a few curved balls and see how they deal with the problems or wobbles and only when you are 100% convinced of their commitment to you and your music do your deal with them. Choose carefully. You could be working with this person for the next twenty or so years of your life, which is a lot longer than most people stay married these days.

I believe it is better to have no manager at all than to have the wrong manager.

What do you need from your manager? You need someone who shares your vision and belief in your music. They have to be able to deal with a lot of different kinds of people. On numerous occasions you are simply not going to have the time to meet every single person who is involved in your career. You're not going to be able to sit in every marketing meeting and even if you have the time you should still avoid them like the plague. There's just not the time to meet all of the German licensees, let alone the licensees of the 50 other territories you may be lucky enough to have your records released in, but you are still going to need to be represented on these occasions. If your representative acts like an egotistic moron I'm afraid you're going to be tarred with the same brush and the bottom line in this business is that there are just so many people queuing up for these people's time and attention and money that you put one foot wrong and you go to the back of the queue. Just in case you're thinking, 'Oh well I'll have to wait until I get to the front of the queue again for my turn to come around again' don't! Don't even dream of that, it never happens.

In a manager you need someone who can rally the troops around you. You need someone who can be firm and decisive and can cut through all the crap and hype and bullshit this business throws up daily. You need someone who can just as easily be Mr Nice Guy as someone who is capable of throwing the full Corgi wobble when necessary. The half-Corgi is the manager sitting up on hind legs, front paws paddling as if in water and lots of barking. The full Corgi is where any hint at politeness is immediately dispensed with and the manager goes straight for the jugular. You need someone who can scrub up well for certain occasions. Someone who can hold a conversation with complete strangers beyond discussing football and the weather. Someone who realises that there are times to party and times not to party. Most importantly, in case you missed it first time round, you need someone who has a vision for you, your music and your career.

And the big question is: how much will you have to pay your manager? The quick answer is 20%. Around a fifth of you earnings will go to a manager. Now there are numerous variations on this. Some managers will demand 25%, which doesn't mean you should agree to it. Other (apparently) more reasonable managers will have a commission rate of 15% and again it doesn't necessarily mean you should agree to pay it. It's rather low and you want your manager to be exactly that, your manager, and to donate all their time and energy to you. If he's receiving a mere 15% commission from you he may be tempted to take on other artists as well which, as we'll discuss later, may not necessarily be in your best interest.

To me it always seemed fair that a manager should take 20% gross on records (obviously after recording costs and all the deductions you, the artist, are subject to) and publishing because it's clear profit for the artist but you might want to try and get them to take 15% or 20% of the nett of your live earnings, i.e. after you've paid all your on-the-road expenses. I suppose the fairest way to look at it is that you should be looking to your manager to be taking commission on what you take home, not what you are turning over.

3. A Wee Chapter About The Big Pie

I suppose before we go into who can help you achieve your success you should examine where your (financial) success will come from.

Records

There are two main sets of income from your records.

A) The person or persons who perform on the records, i.e. the recording artist, receive record royalties. It works out at about 30p per single and about £1.20 per album.

B) The person or persons who wrote the song, i.e. the songwriter, will receive songwriting royalties, somewhere in the region of 51p per album.

A & B need not necessarily be one and the same. In the case of Bob Dylan, The Beatles, Ray Davies, Paul Simon and Van Morrison where the performer is also the writer, obviously it is. But in the case of say, the majority of boy bands, girl bands, combos (boy and girl bands), Bob The Builder, Cliff Richard and Elvis Presley they are not. I mention both Elvis and Cliff though just to show that you need not necessarily record your own work to be mega successful.

So every time a record is sold the performing artist will receive a small payment (minus deductions which we'll go into later) and the songwriter will receive a small payment. On top of which every time the record is played on the radio, television and stage a small payment will find its way back into the performer's pockets and writer's pockets via the various collection societies, PRS, PPL, GVL, Amadi and Sami.

Now say your act has a hit record with a song written by an external writer, if someone else chooses to record (cover) the same song and it's successful the second time around (as well) then your act will not receive an additional penny. All of the new income will go only to the writer. (Obviously the second performer will receive their record royalties but will not share any of the songwriter royalties.) Unless of course you are Nanci Griffith and you record a beautiful song, 'From A Distance,' written by someone else, Julie Gold. Nanci loved the song so much she had the foresight to sign it to her own publishing company and then when she made it popular other people such as Bette Middler and Cliff Richard recorded it and had successful versions. These new versions earned both Nanci and Julie additional income.

But back to your records. Every time one of your songs is used in a movie or for an advert, the record company and the publishing company will be paid a bunch of money (sometimes as much as £100,000 each). Depending on your deal, a certain amount of this will make its way back to the writer (via music publisher) and to the performer (via the record company).

Live Income

For concert appearances you will receive income and we'll go into the breakdown of that later, i.e. where the money comes from and where it goes.

Television & Radio Appearances

Not a lot of income here I'm afraid. For instance for an appearance on *Top Of The Pops* a four-piece group will be paid, in total, about £500. It will cost just as much in expenses for them to do the show. Once you hit the Celebrity A-list then a different set of television shows will become available to you and most of them do tend to pay top dollar, particularly those on the European mainland.

Mostly though all TV and Radio appearances, if you're lucky enough to get them, are gold dust in that they are treated as promotional vehicles which will help you sell lots of records and if you sell lots of records then check the Records section, listed above.

Merchandising

When you go into Woolworth's and you see all those millions of Spice Girl dolls lying around the shelves it means two things. It means that someone has done a deal on The Spice Girls' behalf for a particular company to manufacture and distribute the said goods and to pay the all-singing, all-dancing, all-smiling girls large wads of dosh for the privilege. The second thing is that the particular merchandising company in question is going to be pissed off. You see the fact you've seen so many dolls lying around the shelves of Woolies means that it hasn't been a successful endeavour and the said company is going to have lost quite a few bob.

Swag is the term used to describe the merchandising you will see on sale at the concert venue. Items like, T-shirts, baseball caps, sweat shirts, posters, brochures, patches, transfers, badges, keyrings, pens and tour jackets will all have the band's logo and will be on sale at quite high prices. The majority of successful touring artists make a very healthy income from their swag. Ticket holders at the concert will hand over anything from £2.50 to £16.00 per person for their souvenirs. If we're talking about a concert at Wembley Arena, with a capacity of 10,000 (plus) that's certainly enough to keep your manager in fine claret for a couple of months.

Sponsorship Deals

This is when a rather large company will pay tons of money to you because of your high media profile, just so that their product can be associated with your name. This can be as little as £25,000 on the low end and into the millions on the high end. We're talking here about sponsors like Pepsi and Volkswagen. The rule of thumb here is these people usually only want to pay you this money when you, in theory, don't need it. I mean when do any of us not need money? When you need money most, i.e. when you are starting off your career in the music business, sponsors will be as rare as a silent roadie.

Those are your main areas of income although if you're like Sting and Tom Waits and you break into movies you can also expect a nice bit of change from Hollywood. Also if, as a by-product of making your own records, you build your own recording studio, you can receive additional income (not to mention nightmares) from renting your facilities to other artists.

Now you know where your income is going to come from we'd better start you on your way to earning it.

4. The Road From Your Bedroom To Wembley

Your first audience will invariably be the mirror in your bedroom – a good if somewhat indiscriminate start – but you are definitely on the right track. The point I'm trying to make is that you must always get your music, songs and act together away from the public glare.

Okay, you've written your first few songs and that is a great place to start. It's a much better place to start than staring enviously as someone on TV singing what you feel is a doggy song and making (you think) lots of dosh doing so. In all of this, the single most important thing is the bunch of songs you start with. Find something you need to say about love, about life, about politics, about… mushrooms… about anything, anything at all just as long as it is something that moves you. Then find your own set of musical colours to set your lyrics to. Craft your songs, make every word count and do it all when the song is new to you. It's pretty difficult to go back and rewrite lyrics later. Most lyricists say that when the song is first taking shape is the easiest time to keep going over and over it, changing a verse here, a word there. Get in, say what you want to say and get out as soon as possible. It worked for The Beatles, it'll work for you.

For the sake of our very essential book, let's assume you've got your songs together. The next thing you have to think about is how you intend to perform them. Your options are to go solo or with a band. Well it's not strictly true that those are your only two options if you write songs. The third applies when you only want to be a songwriter and not a performer. In that case you don't need an agent, just make a demo tape and send your songs to a music publisher. But, assuming you have ambitions to be a performer as well as a writer, then solo is obviously the most cost-effective way to start. The wage bill is relatively small and you're not going to bitch at yourself for not paying yourself your own money on time. However, if you do intend to work solo you are leaving a lot of the interpretation of your music to the imagination of the music business. I wouldn't do that if I were you. Even if you don't want to have a democratic band you should still consider using a few other musicians to flesh out your sound so that the version of your music that people get to hear is as close to the finished version of your music that you hear in your head. If you are forming a band then it's much easier for you at this stage – your problems come later.

Choosing a professional name is probably the next important part of the process. The name for your group is important, but probably not vitally important. I remember sitting down with John Isley and David Knopfler and trying to convince them that they might want to change the name of their group. This, you understand, was at the beginning of the punk movement and the guard was about to change again. The band in question were very polite, civilised gentlemen and had more in common with Ry Cooder and JJ Cale – whom we represented – than the then current brash thrashers. Luckily enough John and David's band ignored my advice and went on to sell a few records. Oh, by the way, the band in question is Dire Straits and they became so big they even had their own postal code. As it turned out we did help them get a few of their early gigs but we didn't take them on. They didn't have a manager at the time and so they didn't want to sign an agency contract. From an agent's point of view the golden rule is: no contract, no phone calls. We did however, as promoters, do their shows in Ireland and, years later, we organised a tour for Mark Knopfler's splinter group, The Notting Hillbillies. But back to the plot…

So you have your name, you have your songs, you have your musicians, now it's time to start rehearsing and rehearsing and then rehearsing a wee bit more. Around the time boredom is setting in you should plan your first appearance, say for three months ahead. It will be that goal that will see you through the additional three months of rehearsals. For your first performance you should pick somewhere off the beaten path and invite only friends, family and lovers. If you're an out-of-work musician you are going to be pretty low on the first and last of those three categories so make sure there's at least one Irish member in your group to ensure you'll have a big crowd from the family section.

Do your gig and have fun. That's the important part of all of this, have fun. If you're having fun and enjoying what you do it tends to be pretty infectious and so there's a good chance the audience will have fun too. Oh yes and record the gig. Don't bother to use the Rolling Stones Mobile unit, if indeed it still exists. Something cheap and cheerful will do.

"Do we get to have an agent now?" the group all shout in perfect harmony – well they would, wouldn't they, after all those rehearsals and a gig?

"No!"

"Do we send out copies of the live tape we made of last night's show to everybody in the music business?"

"No."

"Do we get to make a demo now?" the group all shout, the harmonies wavering a little after those two bits of disappointing news.

"No!"

"No?"

"No!"

"What do we do then?" the group all whisper, harmonies all out the window by this stage.

Well you return to your rehearsal room and go through the live tape song by song, listening as closely to the audience's reaction as to the performance of the songs. Audiences never lie. They can't. No matter how enthusiastic they may want to be because they know you, when you listen to their applause on a tape you will hear very clearly which songs worked and which songs didn't. Start rehearsing again and then, just like last time, put another show in for say two or three months down the line. If you were really happy with the quality of your first performance this time expand the audience beyond your immediate group of friends. Hire the upstairs or back room of a pub. You'll be surprised at how reasonable landlords will be when they realise you are going to bring 10, 20, 30, 50, 100 drinkers into their pub. Print flyers and tickets. I bet at least one member of your band will be a computer genius and she, or he, will have a computer programme that will print up multicoloured flyers. Keep them simple. Keep them classy and try and find a way to include a few hints in art and words that will bring across something about the essence of your music. Throw a bit of mystery in there as well – that always works wonders. Have your band and all of your mates sell tickets to all of their mates. It's the networking theory and it's been proven to work wonders.

In your spare time find a way to get a bit of studio experience. Go to the nearest recording studios tell them you'll make the tea, you'll sweep the floor, you'll remove the prog rock band Yes' fake green grass, wooden cows and wooden trees from the studio after they leave. Do absolutely anything; even say you'll work for free. Anything, just as long as you can get in there and see how a recording studio works. Save your home recording experiments until later. Latch on to an engineer and be his runner, assistant, anything (well nearly anything remember this is the music business we're talking about) just so you can get a chance to see him in action with a real group. See if you can hang on part time for about six months or so and learn, learn and then learn some more.

At the same time as you're rehearsing, selling tickets for your next show, writing songs and getting studio experience, see if you can also get some work as a roadie. Either with Stage Miracles, who supply all the load-in and load-out teams for the majority of the London promoters or, preferably, go on the road as a roadie with a professional band. Use the opportunity to get your hands dirty and see how things really work from the inside. Pretty soon you will realise all is not as it might seem. The politics of a band on the road are intriguing and if you know what to expect later… Well, forewarned gives you an extra couple of arms.

"Okay, our second show is successfully under our belt. Now do we get an agent?"

"No."

"What? Well at least do we send off our live tapes to everyone?"

"No."

"No? Ah for feck sake, come on."

Okay, here's one of the big secrets coming. Record companies, agents, managers are all alike – they like to discover their acts. They like to tap into something already in existence. Remember Spandau Ballet? No, not my particular cup of tea either, but they did have 10 hit singles including 1 number one, 5 top 10 albums including one which hit the top spot in the charts, and they did play a blinder at the start of their career. They, decked out in their various New Romantic kits, used to play special events like the ones I was telling you about. They got their shit together, songs, music, sound and image, and they played only private functions and parties that they organised. Not particularly revolutionary – the Kinks used to do it in the 1960s – but very effective. They created their own little scene and started to develop a following. Then they had friends of friends drop the word into key record company executives' ears, "Pssst, you want to get down to the One Legged Fox and Goose and check out this amazing new group."

It works every time. The key words are "check" and "out," but they have to be used together.

The record executive goes through his 10 million demo cassettes and can't find any of their music. He goes down to the gig and finds executives from all of his competitors already there and he thinks, "How come they're already onto this?" The obvious answer is that the friends of friends have been very effective in spreading the word – but our executive, let's call him Malcolm, he's not to know that. He just sees all these other people and immediately he's interested and that's before the group even come on the stage.

So you have your audience, you have your sound, you have your look, you have the ears of the music industry and now it's down to you and to your songs. And the magic of doing it this way is that you don't have to play every dive in England, 3rd on the bill, then 2nd on the bill and rarely top of the bill, to get started. That's certainly the way it used to happen, but it rarely happens that way anymore. These days it's just as effective, and a lot less expensive, to play one key date a month just as long as you make the date work for you. If you have everything in place and your act together (figuratively and artistically speaking) you'll get your record deal and be on your way. But please remember you are just another step on your way. A lot of people make the mistake of thinking that once they have a record deal, they are made. Not so. It's important if you go the above route that you don't forget the audience you have started to build up, keep working at it, maybe spread your wings a little further afield and develop other areas so that you are not overplaying your strong area. The important part in all of this is to try and have an audience waiting for your first record by the time it comes out. That way you have a head start on the majority of acts.

Around this time you'll probably have gone as far as it's possible to go without an agent. If you've done all of the above you'll certainly be gaining their attention.

5. This Is Where I Come In

Agents do everything and they do everything because they have to. Most of the time when we take on a new act it's too early for a manager to be involved. So you have to either help out or watch your new hopefuls go down the pan.

You see when I first started there weren't all the clear divisions between the professionals that there are now. Basically you had two groups of people, those who made the music and those who helped those who made music perform their music. I became involved with my first group when I was about 12 years old. They were The Blues By Five (five people who played the blues, get it?) and they were all my schoolmates. Three of them could play the guitar (one (literally) drew the short straw and switched to bass), one whose dad had a car and could drive his kit around for him played drums, and the one whose parents were rich enough to afford to buy a microphone and an amplifier was the singer. And me? I was a big fan of Hank Williams and Ray Charles but I didn't have an ounce of music in my body so playing any instrument was definitely out. I do remember spending a month or so trying to master playing the bagpipes but then I thought if I had all that wind to spare there must be some better use to put it to! My five mates had their band and spent a lot of time rehearsing, and even a greater amount of time talking about how big they were going to become. In order to continue to hang around with them I had to find a way of doing something that involved me with the group. At that point I lived two doors away from a professional musician who played in a local showband.

Irish showbands played the Irish ballroom circuit. Actually some of them ended up in Scotland so they must have taken a wrong turn at Larne – but that's another ferry tale. The ballrooms were open three nights a week from 8.00 p.m. until 2.00 a.m. One of the problems the showbands had was that the pubs didn't close until about 11.00 p.m. and so the ballrooms didn't fill up until about 11.30 p.m. The showbands didn't want to play to an empty ballroom so they developed this scenario where groups, called relief groups, would play to nobody for three hours. Then, just before the midnight hour, the venue would miraculously fill up and the relief group would get to play to a couple of thousand people for three songs. Hearts beating faster than a Lanberg drum they would then make way for the showband. It was the breeding ground for all the young musicians who didn't particularly want to join a showband.

As I say, I lived three doors up from this professional musician – he played Saxophone and was called Dixie Kerr, and a fine man he is too – so it was decided that I would speak to Dixie on behalf of The Blues By Five to see if they could play a few dances as relief group to Dixie's showband, the Breakaways. He said, "Yes," and started me on the show business road. The booking was confirmed and I became The Manager. We even had business cards printed. The only problem was that at that time we didn't have a telephone in the house and so for the business card I used the telephone number of one of the public telephone boxes that was about half a mile up the road. Which meant when anyone rang looking to book the group… well let's just say they had to wait a wee while. Which wasn't really a major problem as most of the communications was done by snail mail anyway.

So there it is I was The Manager, which in terms of job description meant I had to blag local journalists to write about the group. I'd then blag the journalist to blag his newspaper's photographer to take and print group photographs for free. I had to find somewhere for them to rehearse. I had to look after the money, or lack of it. I had to find gigs (dances). I had to blag friends with cars to drive us and our precious equipment to gigs. I had to help carry in and set up the gear. I had to blag mineral drinks from the ballroom owners. I had to find the ballroom owners when it was time to pick up the fee. Basically, a lot of blagging, as you can see.

Around that particular time of the night, the time to pick up the fee, the ballroom manager would be doing his well-rehearsed disappearing act. When I'd eventually manage to find them I'd have to prize open their hands to extract the money, crumpled note by crumpled note and hot sweaty coin by hot sweaty coin. The conversation might go something like this:

24

"Great night tonight, Sammy."

"There's a lot of people in," Sammy would say.

"Aye, even the balcony is full," I'd say.

"We don't have a balcony, Paul," he'd say.

"Oh, you're right," I'd say, "It just looks like you have a balcony because the audience are standing on each other's shoulders."

"Oh, no need for a balcony here, sure I've got the biggest ballroom in Ireland," Sammy would say.

"Aye, sure with trousers as baggy as those I'm not surprised," I'd say.

"Away with ye," Sammy would say and would stop laughing mid-sentence and become very serious. "Look Paul. What can you do for me on the fee tonight? How's about a wee luck penny?"

"But Sammy, you're packed to the rafters," I'd say in disbelief.

"Aye, I know Paul," Sammy would say, "but we've had a disastrous night on the mineral stall; the place is so packed no one could get near it!"

And you'd both have another laugh and you'd leave with your fee, all of it, unless you were the main act. With their joking about, the ballroom managers were just putting you through the paces of what would happen nightly should you ever progress to becoming a main act.

Following the banter with the ballroom owners you'd try and find your group and driver and pack up the gear and leave. The guitarist would usually be standing at the front of the ballroom, by the stage, on the side of the showband's guitarist, either to make him nervous or to steal some of his licks. The drummer would be chatting up three girls (always). The driver would be bored with it all and would have nipped out to try and find a pub with a faulty lock on the back door. So most nights you'd have to pack the gear yourself or with the help of some of the locals who were attracted to your glamorous world.

But I was hooked, I was hooked on the sounds coming from the stage. It didn't matter if it was showband or a relief group as long as the music they produced was good. I really enjoyed it so I would do whatever was needed to keep my group on the road. I'd have to say the same things are important now as were important then. There are just basic things probably worth noting you don't mess about with.

1. Arrive on time.

2. Ensure in advance all your gear works properly.

3. Keep punctual stage times.

4. Look good. There is a vast difference between dressing up or down to suit a fashion and dressing scruffily.

5. Have a well-rehearsed set. It really does not matter what style of music you choose to play. It matters only that you play it well.

6. Be polite to all those you come into contact with. Apart from anything else, it makes your life a lot easier.

7. Always have plenty of printed promo material (photos, biographies and posters) available.

Now, if you follow all of the above it won't necessarily mean you are going to be successful – that depends entirely on how people react to your music – but it does mean you are going to be noticed and it does mean you're not going to miss opportunities. Okay, it's your turn to say, "But what about Oasis and the Sex Pistols?" And I'd say they were both very clever. I also qualify it by saying appearances can be deceptive or, as Houdini might have said, "Disappearances can be very deceptive."

But that was all about my early stages let's get back to yours.

6. Too Many Moriartys And Not Enough Lone Rangers or, How Does An Artist Find An Agent?

I've just described one way to get started but it's not the only possible route. Let's not forget though that it is a very effective method of launching your act and if you use it, well who knows how big you could become? Hey, perhaps you could even end up in *Eastenders*? You may not want to use this idea but you might want to consider variations on the theme. If you haven't yet found a manager and you can't get to grips with organising and pulling all of the above together by yourself, you may want to find an agent immediately. That way you can enjoy a few shortcuts and you've also got the ideal person to ensure Malcolm the A & R man from the record company and all of his mates come down to see you.

So how do you find your agent?

I've included a list at the end of this book of some of the London agencies. I've included the names of those I feel are some of the best agents around. It's a very personal choice but, if knowing what I know now, I was a manager starting off with a new group, these are the agents I would approach (particularly the first one) to represent my act. Look through the list and see do you, or any of your friends, recognise any of the names.

"Oh look there's Asgard, doesn't that geezer who writes crime novels work there?"

No, I didn't mean recognise like that, although thanks a million for the plug. No, I mean does anyone in your immediate circle know anyone in one of the agencies. You know, know them well enough that they could ring them up and put a word in the agent's (let's call him Arthur) ear to watch out for your demo tape or, even better, to try and get Arthur down and see you next time you perform.

You see, Arthur receives several demos a day and hopefully he will give them all at least a brief listen. But some agents, maybe not Arthur I grant you, don't even bother to listen to the cassettes at all. The best demos to send in should contain four tracks, your best four tracks. Less is more. Spend all your money on four tracks. Remember, this is not meant to be the definitive final recorded version. All you are trying to do is to demonstrate the song to a degree that the listener can hear the potential of your song. If they like your initial four songs there will be lots of other occasions for them to hear the remainder of your material. It's not advisable to send live recordings initially. Like the music, keep your cassette jacket simple: the name of your group; the names of the songs; the names of the songwriter and a telephone number. There is no need to send a large letter describing how the mix isn't the way you like it to be. If you don't like it, don't send it to anyone and throw it in the dustbin. Only send in things you absolutely love. I still get cassettes and CDs sent in with notes saying the new stuff, which will be on the next demo, is much better. Thank you very much but I'd prefer to wait and hear the better stuff.

Arthur shocks you by hearing something on your tape that he likes and he rings you up for a chat. He's looking to check you out. Maybe he comes to a gig and sees what you're like live or maybe he was just checking to see if you have any other demos. Now the equally important thing at this point is for you to use this time to check out him and his office. Too many artists are so happy that someone, anyone, is paying attention and praising their music that they will sign anything with anyone who will come along. Not a good idea. As I mentioned, like with your manager, you could and should have a long relationship with your agent. Chopping and changing offices sends out a certain message. So it helps big time if you actually like your agent. Arthur goes to one of your gigs and he loves it. He hears more songs that he is equally impressed by and he wants to sign you to his agency.

Do you sign a contract? Well I suppose the honest answer to that is if you can get away without signing one then you should try and do that. The problem is that most agents worth their salt will not lift a telephone on your behalf until you've signed on the dotted line. There are a few reasons for that and I'll go into them here in the hope that it will help you make your decision, particularly if you ever come knocking on Asgard's door.

In the perfect world everyone is honourable and when you agree to work together then agree terms, that should be more than enough. Unfortunately the reality is different. Why? Because artists want to keep their options open to see how good the agent is, or they are hoping to eventually find an agent who will be cheaper. Maybe even they are hoping to find a manager and they know that manager may have his own favourite agent. Again, there are variations on these themes.

From the agent's side, the reason every agent worth their salt will require you to sign a contract is because they are going to want to protect their investment and their reputation. No matter how successful an artist is, the agency will run at a loss for at least the first year. In that year, hopefully, the agency will exploit their relationships with promoters on your behalf. The last thing Arthur the agent needs is for the act to then run off to another agency and work with another set of promoters. The next time Arthur rings up his promoters with his next fave rave he's going to get the short shrift because the promoter will have seen one of his competitors reap the rewards of his last investment with the deserting artist. Because there is a chance that the artist might find a manager with his own connections, and because there is always other agents who will represent an artist for a lesser commission, I'm afraid that Arthur will want you to sign on the dotted line.

What's an agent contract like? Well, most of the agency contracts I have seen are a pile of rubbish. They ramble on and on for three or four pages and are very biased on the agent's side. At Asgard we have a simple single-page letter of agreement; basically it covers:

1. The essence of the agreement: Representation for live work.

2. The period covered: Four years.

3. The commission payable: 15% of gross fees.

4. The territory covered: The World.

So, right from the start, everyone knows exactly what they are getting into and there are no excuses acceptable down the line. Once you are up and running and start to achieve reasonable fees, most agents are prepared to renegotiate their commission rate down to 10%. This is, of course, for everywhere except North America and Canada where your UK agent will have to pay an American sub-agent out of his, or her, 15%.

If I was a manager responsible for signing my artist to Arthur, I would ask for a key man clause in my artist's contract. Effectively what this means is, should Arthur ever move to another agency, my act wouldn't be stuck for the remainder of the contractual period with an office who, although not interested in my act anymore, are not honourable enough to let my act go.

It doesn't matter how big an agency is or how great their reputation is, unless there is someone in the office (Arthur in your case) who really cares for you, you are not going to have an equal chance of success. This particularly applies to you if you go the star manager route. The star manager will ensure the agency of his main act will sign you. The agency will be happy to sign you to keep star manager happy. It doesn't, however, mean that the agency will get you enough, or even any, gigs and they will have a list as long as your forearms of justifiable excuses for not getting you gigs. So my advice is: don't sign with an office, sign with an agent.

7. Too Many Oysters Not Enough Pearls or, How Does An Agent Find An Artist?

For my own part I became an agent by accident. I had no great design or master plan. As I mentioned earlier, when I started I was simply helping a bunch of mates get up on stage and play their music. The Beatles came along and turned me, and most of the rest of the world, on and I moved to London thinking that was where the music scene was so that was where I wanted to be.

London in 1967 was a hoot. I had a chance to see and hear first-hand the artists I'd been reading about in the *NME* for the past couple of years. I had no sooner unpacked my bags than I was growing a moustache and making my first pilgrimage up to the West End to the Marquee Club. It seemed to me that there were clubs on every street corner where you could hear music. *Sgt. Pepper's Lonely Hearts Club Band* was the number one album on the charts – it held the top position from 3 June until 14 October – and flower power was in full flow. Tie-dye shirts, granddad shirts, loon pants, Fairisle Sweaters, corduroy shoes and National Health wire-framed glasses were the order of the day. Everything was loud and colourful. Kaftans were very cool. I remember buying one but not being able to pluck up the courage to wear it. I grew up in a community where people would have said, "Who let you out dressed like that?" and it takes a lifetime to outgrow that. People in the music business though still went to work dressed in suits, shirts and ties – there was still the odd gentleman wandering about with bowler hat and brolly – but the lunatics were gradually, and very successfully, taking over the asylum. The other albums in the charts at that point included, *The Sound Of Music*, *Scott* by Scott Walker, *Best Of The Beach Boys*, *Dr Zhivago*, *Fiddler On The Roof*, *Buddy Holly's Greatest Hits* and albums by Tom Jones, Jimi Hendrix, Englebert Humperdinck, and John Mayall. The singles chart from September of that year (1967) probably shows better what was starting to happen musically. We had The Small Faces and their 'Itchycoo Park,' The Rolling Stones pretending they were The Beatles with 'We Love You,' Keith West's 'Excerpt From A Teenage Opera' (did he ever release the full Opera?), Flowerpot Men and 'Let's Go To San Francisco,' The Beach Boys' 'Heroes And Villains,' The Move with 'Flowers In The Rain' (the first ever record to be played on the newly-formed Radio One), The Kinks were between two classics 'Waterloo Sunset' and 'Autumn Almanac,' Traffic's absolute gem 'Hole In My Shoe' was peaking, then you had 'Reflections' from the Supremes and Cliff holding up the old guard with 'The Day I Met Marie.' Radio One was formed under the Government's instruction to the BBC to come up with something as an alternative to the recently-banned, but very healthy, Pirate Radio stations.

When I moved to London first I didn't necessarily want to work in the music business. I didn't know how you would go about doing that. There were no exams you could take, nor were there any qualifications that could gain you access on the fast track to *Ready Steady Go*. I was in London a while and a few of the Irish artists were doing well in London. We're talking about artists like Taste, Skid Row and Thin Lizzy. I was invited to cover their progress for a Belfast newspaper called *Cityweek*. Infrequent articles grew into a weekly column. Then a mate of mine, the guitarist from The Blues By Five, formed a group called Fruupp and he wanted to bring them straight to London. He asked me if I'd get him a couple of gigs in London so that they could get over here and get a manager and a record deal and live happily ever after. Five years, four albums and a thousand gigs later they still hadn't found a manager and I was doing that along with being their agent, roadie, sound engineer and lyricist – basically they couldn't afford anyone else. In the 1970s, record companies didn't throw large advances at groups – well at least they didn't throw a large one at us – so we lived from, and on, the road. The main spin-off for me, although I didn't realise it at the time, was that I was gaining first-hand experience of all the venues around Europe. I'd meet and look in the one good eye of most promoters on the circuit, which I suppose gave me the best experience necessary for being an agent. On top of which I'd found something I really enjoyed doing.

Becoming an agent is one thing. Finding your first act is slightly more complicated. As an agent the only thing you have is your reputation and your reputation is based to some degree on the acts that you represent. People (incorrectly) think if Arthur represents someone a big as Sliced Pan (today that would be Sliced Pan feat Mrs Williejohn Ross' eldest son JoJo) then he can do a good job for me. Fruupp split up to a tidal wave of indifference so there I was an agent without any artists. Eventually you persuade a group to work with you, in my case it was The George Hatcher Band (affectionately know as The Margaret Thatcher band) and we found them lots of gigs and then a few more gigs and the chap at George Hatcher's record company – Andrew Laurder was his name (it still is his name, in fact) – noticed that we were getting George lots of gigs and he'd just signed a new band and he thought maybe we could do the same job for his new group. His new group were called the Buzzcocks and we did manage to fill their date sheet over the next few years when they enjoyed eight chart singles, one chart EP and three chart albums. It was just as well they'd all that success to celebrate because they certainly liked their champagne did the Buzzcocks. Just because we'd done the Buzzcocks, the Undertones were receptive to our advances and then Penetration, Human League, The Gang Of Four and The Lurkers all followed shortly thereafter.

And the point in telling you this is that it's that easy, or that hard, to become an agent.

From an agent's point of view, artists fall into two main categories. The first is new artists, who you are continuously looking for, and the second are the established artists whose music you love. I was a major fan of Jackson Browne, Nick Lowe, The Blue Nile, Van Morrison, Tom Waits and Ray Davies before I got a chance to work with them.

In fact I remember back in Ulster, hitching up to The Embassy Ballroom in Derry to try and meet the manager and blag a booking for The Blues By Five. (Don't forget an in-person visit is worth a dozen phone calls.) The manager was present in the ballroom and he was routining GoGo dancers – at least that's what I think he was doing but for some reason or other he seemed to have to keep cleaning his glasses and mopping his brow a lot. The piece of music he was using for the girls to do their routine was 'Waterloo Sunset' by the Kinks. I'd already thought that particular single was a classic but 30 plays (that day) later I was convinced it was the work of a genius, so you can imagine how thrilled

I was when 25 years later I got to meet and work with the songwriter in question, Mr Ray Davies, and his band The Kinks.

It's funny, but not a coincidence I feel, that two of the most professional artists I've work with came out of 1960s groups: Ray Davies from the Kinks and Van Morrison from Them. The tickets and records and T-shirts are not sold by accident. It is a business and the core business has to be taken care of. You must earn a reputation for putting on a professional show: always tour with a top quality sound system; have tasty but not overbearing lights; look good; appear on stage punctually; play your hit/hits (delete as appropriate) unbegrudgingly; play a full set; and meet and sign autographs for your fans. When you've won this reputation then your audience will stay with you forever and I do mean forever – Cliff Richard sells every ticket he puts on sale and that's a hell of a lot more tickets than he was selling in the 1950s and 1960s. Van Morrison works to packed houses continuously year in, year out. Same for Ray Davies. I've seen very few artists who consistently send the crowd home with a smile on their collective face the way Ray Davies does. Bob Dylan still plays a staggering 150 concerts per year all over the world, all of which sell out.

The live career of other seemingly more popular artists depends on whether or not they have a single in the charts. If they have, they're fine. If they haven't, then it's hard work. It's not that the record-buying audience turn off from the artists; it's more that the Radio does, and if you're not on the radio, no matter who you are, it's pretty impossible for your audience to be aware of your current music. If you intend to make a career out of making and performing music, all your early moves and decisions are vitally important and professionalism is the key. (Providing, of course, you've got the songs that people react to.)

There is no single way that an agent can find an act. Take Van Morrison for instance. I got my break with him just because I was a fan of his, had been a fan since the Them days. Around the time of the *Wavelength* album, we (Asgard) were negotiating with the UK Management to tour Van in his homeland – we used to do a lot of shows in Ireland. We'd set up two shows in Belfast, three in Dublin and one in Cork. Then we received the news that the UK-based manager was no longer the manager. Through the record company we found out that Van had appointed a new American manager and we got in touch with them and tried to continue the talks. We were advised that it would be impossible for Van to come over just to play in Ireland.

"Okay, we'll do concerts for you in the UK as well," we said, gulping large dollops of air because we'd never promoted a UK tour before.

"Okay make us an offer," they said.

They further advised us that they would have to entertain offers from several UK promoters. Now every single person I knew had a copy of *Astral Weeks* – that may say more about my friends than the popularity of the music, but I didn't think so. I'd also a few mates who worked in record stores (mainly Music Land in Berwick Street) and they had told me that *Astral Weeks* had been the biggest-selling import album ever. So we made our offer for Van to play three nights at Hammersmith Odeon (3,400 tickets per night) while our competitors were offering The Venue (one of Branson's early properties now closed but with only a 640 capacity).

So we got the tour, which included the original six shows in Ireland, three in London and another dozen or so shows around the UK. The entire tour sold out the first day it went on sale and, for me, it was the beginning of an 8-year working relationship with Van Morrison. That first tour I worked on finished in Newcastle and the tour bus returned to London immediately after the concert. Van sang Beatles songs, Beach Boys songs, Hank Williams songs, country classics walking up and down the aisles of the bus. He even took requests on the long drive from Newcastle to London, a very enjoyable experience for those on board. Yes, Van Morrison acting as a human jukebox on the return journey from Newcastle is my lasting memory of that tour.

Now because we represented Mr Morrison, when we approached other artists the doors opened a bit more easily. I'd been a fan of Jackson Browne since his very first album. I loved his voice and I loved his songwriting even more. He made records, which for me were just perfect. I'd been to see him live in concert a few times and played his album *For Everyman* every waking hour God sent me. The record company had brought him over to England once but from what I could gather he didn't have an agent and so I started to track him down. His manager would have polite conversations but the hub of the matter was that he was starting to be mega in America and there was more than enough work for him to do there. I politely pushed on, advising them that with a few well-planned tours he could be mega this side of the Atlantic as well. Then I did the Van Morrison tour and someone in Van's camp (tour manager) knew someone in Jackson's camp and the next time I rang up they were more receptive. Five months later, Jackson Browne was on a 7-week tour of Europe. Can you imagine being able to hear one of your favourite artists live every night (well nearly) for 7 weeks?

One of the partners in Jackson Browne's management company turned out to be one of the managers of Crosby, Stills and Nash and Jackson Browne is a very good friend of Graham Nash. Within a year of the Jackson Browne tour we were touring Crosby, Stills and Nash around Europe. Sadly Mr Crosby was still a bit of a casualty in those days. Not, I hasten to add, during the time he was on stage – for that hour and a half every night he sang as sweetly as a bird – but it was depressing to see (up close) how effectively chemicals can wreck a life. Happily, all his friends rallied around him and by the next time they toured Europe he was a different person, different insofar that when you looked into his eyes you could see someone looking back at you.

At Asgard we've been lucky enough to work with some of the world's greatest Blues artists over the years. I'm talking about people like John Lee Hooker, Buddy Guy, Taj Mahal, Robert Cray and Sonny Terry and Brownie McGee. We represented Sonny Terry and Brownie McGee towards the end of their career together. I remember my very bizarre first meeting with them. Although I'd been through all the tour details in advance with their American representative in New York City, the artists insisted on meeting with me at their hotel the minute they arrived in London. I sat down with them. Sonny, who was probably the best blues harp player who ever lived, was a big, gentle, warm, smiling man and Brownie I always felt was somewhat underrated as a blues artist. Maybe he also felt that to be the case because he was always a little guarded, withdrawn even. Anyway, I sat down with them and as requested went through the tour details with them: the cities; the venues; and of course the fees and the state of the deposits. All artists are keen to ensure that 50% of their fees have been deposited with their agents before stepping on stage for the first concert.

Brownie asked me a few questions as we went along and then just when I thought we'd covered everything Sonny started to ask me all of the same questions over again and had me repeat the fees. You see, they hadn't actually spoken to each other for about 17 years by the time I met them. And that was the funny thing, for although they would never allow any meetings to take place unless they both were in attendance they insisted that you address them both separately and directly. It mattered not that they got to hear the information twice, it was only important that you addressed them as individuals.

I still find it quite incredible that two artists could work together for 17 years, never communicate with each other but still gel so brilliantly on stage. As I mentioned, the shows we did with them were at the end of their career but I was dumbstruck at the power they generated on stage every night.

The other thing I remember about this remarkable duo was that while away from home, every single meal they ate – breakfast, lunch and dinner – they always ate together. I suppose this was as a safeguard against one of them doing a separate side deal with a promoter. Even more incredible was the fact that each and every one of those meals consisted of chicken as a main course.

"Safest food Paul," Sonny would howler. "Safest food in the whole wide world."

Nothing beats the in-person approach. A face-to-face meeting with an American manager or artist is worth about two dozen faxes or phone calls. Tom Waits is another artist I am a big fan of and I had tried on several occasions in the 1970s and 1980s to represent him as an agent. I'd just be starting to develop a relationship with his manager when he would become the ex-manager. Every time I visited Los Angeles I would meet with someone or other about the possibility of representing Tom Waits. One year I was in Los Angeles. As ever, when I found myself with time to kill between meetings I'd head off to Tower

Records on Sunset Boulevard for a good old browse. The minute I entered the vibrant record store I spied all the promo material for *One From The Heart*, which was a soundtrack album Tom Waits and Crystal Gayle had just released.

I'd already seen the movie and loved the music so I immediately asked one of the assistants for a copy of the album.

"Oh, we're very sorry, sir, we've sold out of that particular album," the shop assistant replied. She dropped to a conspiratorial whisper as she continued, 'In fact, I just sold our last copy to Tom Waits himself and he's standing... don't look now... just behind you."

She smiled awkwardly gesturing with her eyes and nose to my left.

I casually browsed in his direction and when I was close enough to make eye contact I introduced myself, "Hi. I'm Paul Charles from Asgard in London and I've been trying to work with you for several years."

Sometimes you've got one shot and one shot only and your have to make your pitch simply and quickly. Tom and his wife Kathleen had heard of my efforts and were very friendly and we retreated to a nearby café for a cup of tea and a chat. One hour or so later I was their agent.

The first tour I did with Tom Waits was a treat, a real treat in every sense of the word. With Tom Waits you not only get to book the show and hear magic music every night, you also get to help put the show together and stage it nightly. My additional duties were to make rain fall on the stage every night at the appropriate time and to figure out how to make a bright light shine on Tom's face from inside his raggedy top hat. The former we perfected on the third night of the tour using a cardboard box filled with small pieces of polythene set up in the lighting rig and attached to a piece of string the other end of which was in my hand. The latter, the beam of white light, however took until the very last concert to master, but master it we did.

The Blue Nile, John Lee Hooker, Roy Orbison, Paul Brady, Mary Black, Christy Moore, Gerry Rafferty, John Prine, John Sebastian and Nick Lowe were all artists whose music I was a big fan of before I'd a chance to work with them. I suppose the point I'd like to make is that I rave about them not because I am lucky enough to work with them; it's more a case that I wanted to work with them because they are great artists and all, without exception, have a little bit of an edge on the live side. I'm still sucker for the live performance.

The reason I recalled those few examples is because they demonstrate I think, that as an agent, you need to do what you do as best you can and hopefully it will serve you well. We've certainly been lucky enough to work with some of my heroes and there are still several artists who I'm a big fan of and would like to work with.

The other main category of artists is new artists, who you pick up at the beginning of their career. For me these were people like Nanci Griffith, Robert Cray, The Roches, Stevie Ray Vaughan, Irish Dement, The Buzzcocks, The Undertones, The Human League and Hothouse Flowers. These artists are all out there waiting for us and as an agent you are turned on to them by friends, record companies, other artists and cassettes in your mailbag. All you need to do is to have the ears to listen to them, the eyes to see them and the power of your conviction. People generally are passionate about their music and equally, usually, dispassionate about music they don't like. Passion is infectious. When, as an agent, you discover a new act you start on a mission to convince as many people as possible that the artist is brilliant. You ring up a promoter and rave about an artist, he'll (hopefully) think about all the other artists you've (hopefully) been correct about and he'll be prepared to take a chance by joining you in the age-old promoter/agent partnership of helping to find an audience for the artist. If he's as convinced as you are then he'll go off and vibe up all of his contacts, eventually getting that vibe through to the public.

A friend of mine in America sent me a copy Nanci Griffith's first album. This particular friend, a musician, was not involved in Nanci's career in any way. As they say in the business, there was no percentage in it for him but he thought I might like her music. He was 100% spot on. I loved it. I made contact with her manager and did a deal to bring her over. On her first visit she sold 74 tickets out of 100 in the Mean Fiddler Acoustic Room. The album sold a couple of thousand copies. She returned to Ireland and England quite a few times over the following several years until she regularly had Gold Albums in the UK and

Ireland and because of the strength of her live show she could sell out a week at the Olympia Theatre in Dublin (7,000 tickets in total) and three nights in The Royal Albert Hall in London (15,000 tickets in total). Robert Cray was another artist whose career and record sales were driven and led by his success in concert venues up and down the country. As was the case with all of the above artists although people like Hothouse Flowers and The Undertones also enjoyed several top 10 singles as well.

Thankfully the live scene is not a scene that fades. We are currently starting out artists like Jack L, Eric Bibb, Lisa Ekdahl and Kelly Joe Phelps on this circuit. So the artists are still out there, waiting for managers and agents and record companies. It's up to us to find them. It's always better to find your own though. Don't try to shortcut your agent career by nicking other agents' artists. Which brings us back quite nicely to our contract issue. As an agent, always sign your artist never sign the manager. The manager may get fired or make so much money he retires, so always make your contract directly between you and the artists.

8. Another Music In A Different Kitchen

Thanks to Shelly for the title of this chapter, that's the Buzzcocks' Pete Shelly of course. It seemed appropriate because I wanted to talk about the non-music acts I've worked with.

Occasionally – well, once, to be precise – my two careers have overlapped. I've been a book collector, particularly of British Detective Fiction for years. That's how I got into writing in fact. Anyway I used to see Colin Dexter when he did book signings and readings and I found him to be hilarious. He is funny because he has complete and absolute understanding and control of the English language. He would have his gatherings in stitches by being genuinely funny. After one of these evenings I thought he would be perfect for 'An Evening with' kind of presentation. I approached his agent who passed on my request. Apparently Mr Dexter was amazed that I thought anyone would turn up to see and hear him speak but he'd like to meet me.

We duly met and I explained my idea to him. I told him that we (Asgard) would like to present him in a West End theatre talking about his work, life and, of course, Morse. His main concern was about who, if anybody, would turn up. You see, when authors do book readings and signings such events are invariably held in bookstores and have no admission charge. In fact, sometimes the publisher will even stand for a glass or two of wine for those who do bother to turn up. Obviously if we went into a West End theatre with Mr Dexter we would have to charge for the tickets. Eventually I convinced him that he would enjoy the company of a large, if not full, house and he agreed to proceed.

We booked The Duke of York's Theatre in St Martin's Lane and went back to Mr Dexter with the usual requirements of the music business, i.e. the capacity, the gross and the offer of a fee plus a percentage. Unlike the majority of the music business – sorry make that the entire music business – Mr Dexter looked at my figures and at my offer for a fee and said words to the effect that he couldn't possibly accept such a fee and wanted only (approximately) half of what I was offering. Did I agree? Does a bear do a number two in the woods?

'A Conversation With Colin Dexter' was the original, if somewhat obvious, title we came up with and we took our adverts and printed the posters and put the performance on sale. Surprise, surprise, it sold phenomenally well and Mr Dexter made all the money I'd originally offered and a few bob on top in the percentage. In advance of the show he'd been slightly nervous about what he was going to talk about to fill the time and we agreed that for the first 40 minutes or so he would talk about his life, work and Morse, and then he'd take questions from the audience. The first section flew by and the 40 minutes became 75 minutes and the few questions from the audience became another 40 minutes. It was a thoroughly enjoyable evening.

The main difference between Mr Dexter and the majority of my other clients was that where they are young and keen to get on the road and stay on the road Mr Dexter has hit 70 years of age and harbours no such desire. We did however present 'A Conversation With Colin Dexter' for a few nights at the Edinburgh Festival where he repeated his London success.

My ventures outside of the music business though have been few and far between. I prefer to stick to what I know. However, I can remember a bit of a buzz starting around town about a certain bunch of alternate comedians who were doing late-night weekend shows at the small theatre in Raymond's Revue Bar in London's trendy Soho. I visited the theatre for one of the midnight shows. ("Honest, your honour. That's what I was doing in Soho at midnight. I was there on office business.") I was shocked to find the queue snaked its way around the vibrant streets. Not one of the artists on the bill – Twentieth Century Coyote, The Outer Limits, Arnold Brown and two very weird girls called French and Saunders – could have been, by any stretch of the imagination, called household names, but here they were packing out show after show, weekend after weekend. Oh yes and the show was MCed by a very young and fresh faced Ben Elton. He was still travelling by bicycle so he hadn't quite developed his motor mouth routine. I enjoyed the entire performance, particularly Twentieth Century Coyote, who were probably the best live comedy act I'd seen since Ken Dodd. I should probably point out here that I can give no higher praise to a comedy act – I have been to several of Ken Dodd's marathon performances and he makes me laugh until tears flow down my face. Twentieth Century Coyote were in fact Ric Mayall and Adrian Edmondson who were (and still are) side-splitting hilarious. All of the above performers worked under the collective title of The Comic Strip.

I eventually tracked down Peter Richardson (who, with Nigel Planner – Neil from *The Young Ones* – made up The Outer Limits). Peter seemed to have drawn the short straw because he was lumbered with organising The Comic Strip. Over the following months we used various members of the troupe to open up some of our concerts. I have vague memories of a Spinal Tap kind of group called Bad News, which consisted of Twentieth Century Coyote and The Outer Limits, supporting Kate and Anna McGarrigle at The Venue. Eventually the word on The Comic Strip spread to the extent that we were able to book them a college tour of the UK, which was phenomenally successful, the majority of the venues selling out way in advance. Then television (their collective and individual ultimate goal) beckoned and off they went, and kept going and going and going and going. And didn't they do well?

9. The Deal Is What You Make It

Don't worry I haven't forgotten about your band and your career. You're getting closer to some kind of success. Are you getting excited?

Anyway, for the heck of it let's call the band Wire Crates. They have their manager (or not) and they have Arthur. Remember your agent, Arthur? Now you need to pick a lawyer. That's a solicitor to you and me but the music business side of the legal profession like to be known as lawyers, like their American counterparts. Your agent can recommend a few names, and so can your manager. The golden rule is never to choose a solicitor who acts for your manager, your agent or anyone else you are involved with. I'd meet a few people if I were you. I've included a few names at the end of the book. These are all people who specialise in the music business. But, at the end of the day, it really is down to you and how you get on with them. Meet them, chat with them and see if you like them. It doesn't matter how great their reputation is – if you don't like him, or her, don't ask them to work with you. When putting your team together I think it is vital to have at least one person involved who is a constant. Managers may come and go, agents may come and (won't want to) go, but lawyers and accountants should stay once in place. Apart from anything else they get paid by the hour so all the advice they give you will never be based on how much commission they are going to make on a deal. Throughout your entire career you'll find it very comforting to be able to consistently go back to the same person just to run things by them. So, what I'm saying is, try to choose your lawyer, and accountant, with some of the wisdom and expertise you expect from both of them.

You've done a few shows and Malcolm the A&R guy from the record company has started to pay attention. (A&R stands for either 'Artiste & Repertoire' or 'Arrange & Record.' There seems to be two schools of thought as to the origins of the title.) Anyway the A&R guy is the artist's first contact with the record company. He is the guy who spends all his life either in a darkened basement listening to demos or in small dingy clubs listening to groups. He rarely sees the sun! He is the talent scout whose job is to find the talent for the record company to feed into their hungry and expensive machine. Today it's Wire Crates and pretty soon Malcolm and someone from his business affairs department will start to negotiate a deal with you or your representative(s). No matter who your representative(s) may be always take part in these negotiations yourself. Sometimes the buzz of a record company simply being interested in you and being prepared to release your work is enough to ensure you sign on any dotted line which is put in front of you. But we're talking here about your music and quite possibly a big chunk of your life being tied up with Malcolm's company, so force yourself to take an interest and an active part in the negotiations. If your lawyer and the business affairs person start talking in legal gobbledegook don't be scared to say, "Hang on a minute. Could you run that by me again, only this time could I have it in English please."

If you're a new group and you've created a bit of a buzz, your deal memo could read something like:

1. Commitment: One album firm, four further options. Which means that the record company are committing to you for one album, whereas you are committing to them for five.

2. Advance (recoupable against royalties):

£100,000 for first album

£125,000 for second album

£150,000 for third album

£200,000 for fourth album

£300,000 for fifth album.

Sadly, most artists don't bother to read beyond these figures but, for those who do read on, the deal memo will continue.

3. Recording costs: Agreed in advance by the record company and deducted from future royalties.

4. Video costs: Video costs to be agreed in advance by the record company and deducted from future royalties.

5. Territory: The World.

6. Tour support: The shortfall between the fees your receive and the money you have to pay in expenses in order to undertake said tours – to

be agreed in advance by the record company and deducted from future royalties.

7. Duration of contract: Until a year after the fifth album has been delivered.

8. Royalty rate: This doesn't really mean a lot. Record Companies don't mind giving a high percentage and then taking some of it back from you within the contract, so always ask your lawyer or your record company, "how much exactly do I get in my pocket for every album sold?" If the figure is in the £1.20 neighbourhood you're on the right track. But please don't forget that very important question, "But how much money will I be paid for every record I sell?" Tell them you are not in the slightest bit interested in reading paragraph upon paragraph detailing what deductions they can make from your royalties and also tell them you care not a fig about wholesale and retail and packing deductions, and gross and nett and overseas currencies and the price of fish in Kathmandu. In all of this you have to remember that you're new to this. Don't allow them to make you feel intimidated. The record companies have a 50-year head start on you. That's not to say that all of them are out to take advantage. The great ones will try to accommodate you as best they can.

All you need to do in your negotiations is to ensure that the deal is one you will be able to live with. If you are afraid that your record royalty rate is too low, then say so at the meeting. Suggest that they introduce an escalation clause once you achieve your plateau of sales. For instance, if your first album sells 250,000, the record company will have received a fair return on their investment, so in your initial negotiations suggest that they increase your royalty rate by half a percent when you sell 250,000, and then an additional half a percent when you reach 500,000, and maybe an extra one percent at 1,000,000, an extra 2% at 2,000,000 and an even further 2% at 3,000,000. All of which would give you an extra (and realistic) 6% when (and if) you reach three million sales.

We managed Tanita Tikaram. I saw her do her first ever show at the Mean Fiddler in December 1987. By the end of July of the following year she had her first top 10 hit with 'Good Tradition.' I mention it here only because when we were doing the initial negotiations I requested a royalty escalation such as the one I've listed above. When I reached the 3,000,000 figure, Mr Warner and several of his Brothers were rolling about on the carpet in hysterics. Through their tears of laughter they said, "Paul, if Tanita ever achieves 3,000,000 sales, of course we'll pay her that royalty." Within two years of signing the contract, sales of Ms Tikaram's very fine debut album *Ancient Heart* coasted past the 3,500,000 sales figure and Tanita had achieved her superstar royalty. Mind you, she earned each and every penny of it. I know just how hard she worked for her success.

For me, the major imbalance in the deal offered by the majority of the record companies is the issue of who owns the masters. Record companies should pay for the masters if they want to own them. But they never do, do they? Yes, they pay for the master in advance but then they deduct it from your money (royalties). Artists should own their own masters. It's their birthright, their bloodline, whatever you want to call it and if that's not reason enough for you then they should own the master simply because they pay for them. Yes, the record companies can say that they have to pay for the recording of the masters up front, and in fact that's perfectly true. So what you should say is, "Okay, fine you (the record company) can own the masters and pay us a royalty until such time as you've recouped your costs at which point, and for life thereafter, the ownership of the masters reverts to us, the artists, and we will then lease the masters back to you." This is certainly not a situation that will be changed overnight, but if enough artists hold out in the negotiations and for as long as possible then eventually the record companies are going to have to give in on it. And that's the point at which the power will swing back to the artists, where it belongs. It's really as simple as that.

Now don't begin to feel too sorry for the record company with this hammering we're giving them. I've never seen a poor record executive. I have, however, seen lots of poor musicians. When you are doing your deal, remember the top executives in UK record companies are currently receiving anything from £100,000 to £1,000,000 per year plus bonus. When your career is long gone they'll still be earning that kind of money. I find the distribution of funds grossly unfair. I think it's about time a bigger percentage of the income finds its way into the musicians' own pockets or purses, where it belongs.

This is not an issue about money. This is about protecting the money you are generating in what is historically a short shelf life. These are probably issues you'll get around to addressing later on in your career when you've sold a few million albums but it's very important you are made aware of them. If artists keep bringing up these issues in the initial negotiations then, bit by bit, things may change for the better. For now though, let's get back and see how Wire Crates are getting on.

The better A & R chappies will also have a good network of contacts, so they'll be able to put you in contact with managers, agents, lawyers accountants etc. Malcolm will also help you make your record, choosing producers, engineers, studios, musicians and helping you select your songs. Be careful during this process because for some strange reason known only to themselves, record company people tend to think that if a named producer has just had a hit record with Joe Bloggs they'll also be able to make your music a hit. It matters not a lot that Joe Bloggs is heavy metal and you are a sensitive singer/songwriter.

In all of this the thing you've got to be most careful about, the thing you've got to be the most precious about, is your music and the people who work with you in the creative process of putting that music together for a record. Really, you get one chance to get it right and then it's down on tape/vinyl/CD forever and you'll never be able to change it. Success has many fathers and if your music is successful you have a whole army of people ready to jump into the spotlight to take the bow for your success. Conversely, failure is quite simply a fatherless child and will always be entirely down to you the artist.

When Warner Brothers first signed Ry Cooder they signed him with the knowledge that they would have to release a few albums until he broke even and started to cover costs for them. As it turned out, it was about 7 albums before the classic *Bop Till You Drop* turned Ry's account from red to black. These days you get one chance, two if you are very lucky. In fact, the same company released only one Little Village album. I wonder had that anything to do with the fact that the debut album didn't reach the accountants' expectations? Little Village were Ry Cooder's 1990s super group featuring Mr Cooder, Nick Lowe, Jim Keltner and John Hiatt. They made but one album. Figure that one out if you can.

So you've got to be extremely careful with the people you choose to work with you. In the recording process producers are obviously the most important and probably the hardest to find. Take your time. Do your research on the producer. Meet up with them as many times as possible. Try to get to know them as best as you can. You need to be able to assess if they are prepared to help you achieve your artistic goals or if they are going to want to go their tried and tested route because they know (they think) it works. That's part of the magic of having a wee bit of studio experience under your belt by this stage. You're going to know the language. You're not going to be in awe the minute you walk into a room to start your record just because of all the other great albums that have been made there. Also, be careful of the fan route. Sadly, too many artists want to make a record with Nick Lowe just because he produced the best Elvis Costello records. Try to find your own Nick Lowe or George Martin or Tony Visconti or whoever.

Once the album is completed, that's the last you'll hear from Malcolm until either the presentation ceremony of your first gold disc or the ugly subject of remixing rears its ugly head. The remixing scenario generally only happens when your first releases are not as successful as everyone had anticipated. Malcolm will return with a desire to fix it for you. Personally I've always been of the opinion that if it's not in the grooves no amount of remixing is going to fix it. But, you've got to appear willing and anyway let's not be negative so close to the start of your career. Album one from Wire Crates is in the can and for the purpose of this tale let's assume the album has been well received. Before Malcolm whizzes off to A& R someone else he will introduce you to the rest of the team, namely the press department, the radio and TV promotion department and the marketing department. They'll all jump onto your career with unbridled enthusiasm. Please always remember that records do not sell by accident, so in the early stages you should do everything you are offered with a smile on your face.

10. A Short Chapter About Music Publishers

"Our record is recorded. We're about to release it. Do we need a publisher for my music?"

"No!" is the simple answer.

"Why?"

"Because Music Publishers are bankers."

Yes, you did read that correctly. The word does start with the second letter of the alphabet and not the fourth last. Basically, the majority of music publishers give you a bunch of money and they then charge you interest for the privilege.

"Ah come on Paul, that's a bit over the top."

"Nope."

Apart from people like Peter Barnes, Stuart Hornall and Kenny MacPherson, most of the publishing houses do little or nothing for their money. In fact, quite a few of them have been started by record companies as another way to make money from their artists' records. If you can find a Peter Barnes, Stuart Hornall or a Kenny MacPherson who will be interested in pushing you and your career as a songwriter first and foremost great, that's definitely the way to go. If not, don't sign just yet. Release the first record under Copyright Control, which means that the song(s) is registered directly to you and all the publishing income will go directly to you. If that single is any size of a hit that's the time to do your publishing deal, when you're hot. You will receive a much better deal from the publisher, a higher advance and a bigger royalty.

"What can I expect from a publishing deal?" the songwriter in Wire Crates shouts.

If your first song is a hit then anything from £100,000 to £250,000 is not unreasonable. Percentage-wise, most publishers will want to deduct 15% to 20% for the privilege of collecting your songwriting royalties on your behalf and paying you a large chunk of it in advance of course. Some publishers will even drop their share to 10% if you push hard enough and you are hot enough. Either way, the important thing to write into the contract is that all the song rights are returned to you after say five years. This way you keep all of your songs under your control.

And just to set the cat amongst the pigeons, ask them – the publishers that is, not the pigeons – if you can have a share of the black box fund. Such a fund actually exists and it's where all unclaimed royalties and percentages from different collection societies end up. Publishers share out the black box fund amongst themselves. No artist that I am aware of actually participates in this revenue.

11. Never Pay To Play

This is the point in your career where the dilemma of gigging or not gigging arises. If at this stage you hadn't picked up on my earlier suggestion and started to build up your own audience, basically what you now have is an album and no audience. All is not lost. The record will be used to vibe up the industry and you will start to play a few showcases, where the record company will bring down lots of their contacts in the business to show you off. It's around this time that the support tour option will be mentioned.

This is the unhealthy practice where a support act (in this case you) buys their way onto a tour. The record company foots the bill, again as an advance against future royalties, and everybody believes it's a short cut to success. First, audiences avoid support acts like the plague, preferring to remain instead in the theatre bar or a pub around the corner. Secondly, journalists seem to time their arrival at the venue at the exact moment the main act takes the stage. The buy-on can cost as much as £25,000 for a 20-day tour of the UK. On top of which there are hotels, transportation, crew, rehearsals and the crew wedge factor to be paid for. The wedge factor is where you pay the headlining group's sound engineer (the person responsible for the sound the audience hears in the venue), the monitor engineer (the person responsible for the sound the musicians hear on stage) and the LD or lighting designer (who is responsible for changing the lighting patterns on stage). This amounts to around a further £30 per man per night.

I suppose it can be argued that the support group gains experience in their stagecraft. My advice would be to get your stagecraft together somewhere less expensive. The only experience you will gain from this is how to play to half empty halls. That could quite possibly be valuable experience for later in your career when you've passed your peak as it were. In America it's completely different. Audiences are used to two-act and sometimes even three-act bills and so the support artists do get the attention (and the fees) they deserve.

The basic rule of thumb is never pay to play. If your first gig is in a club and you receive a fee of £50 then make sure your expenses come to

£46.01, leaving you with exactly enough change to buy another copy of this Pocket Essential to give to one of your mates. If you manage to get your fee up to £100 or £1,000 or even £10,000, the same thing applies – make sure you have change.

"Oh, come on," I hear you say as you drool in your beer over the thought of the fee. "If I was getting £10,000 of course there would be change. I would be turning a fair old profit."

But when you reach that level, you will find that there is pressure to deliver bigger and better shows. You'll have a road crew with a spending power of its own. You'll have a sound engineer who'll want you to go for the Rolls Royce sound systems. You'll have a lighting designer who'll want you to go for the biggest lighting rig ever taken on the road. Your tour manager will want a couple of assistants, separate sleeper coaches for the band, the band's crew and the sound and lights crew. 2, 3, 4 or 10 articulated trucks will now be required to haul your gear around the country. No, that's not a truck that speaks proper that's a fecking expensive, and rather large, lorry to you and me.

Again, as with the initial record company meeting, make sure you're involved in all of the pre-production meetings where decisions are made regarding all matters related to your tour. Have your people spell out to you how much it's all going to cost. And, if you are lucky enough to be on a £10,000 fee, draw the line under all expenditure once it reaches £9,000. And then just sit back and watch the other £1,000 disappear on contingencies.

For the hell of it let's just do a typical costing for a group who will receive £10,000 per concert.

Income (Per Show)	£10,000

Expenses: (Per Show)	
Management Commission	£2,000
Agent's commission	£1,000
Accountant's fee	£200
Hotels	£1,200

PA Hire	£600	
Lighting Hire	£450	
Crew's Wages	£600	
Band's Wages	£1,000	
PDs	£300	
Truck Hire	£500	
Bus Hire	£500	
Misc.	£1,000	
Total Expenses:		£9,350
Balance:		£650

You can usually do five concerts/gigs per week, so the above costs are based on that, which means for the purposes of this costing I've divided the weekly expenses by five to get the per gig expense figure.

PDs (Per Diems) are the £25/£30 food allowances the band and the crew each receive per day. On top of which, on concert days there will be free catering for you in the venue where your catering rider caters for your every whim.

All the rest is self-explanatory, I hope.

"But only £650 left for the artist out of the ten grand, agh come on!" you scream.

"Sorry, but that's your bottom line," your agent will say if he's a brave man.

"I know," you say. "You've inflated the Miscellaneous Figure to build in a wee bit for the artist, haven't you?"

"Sorry," the agent will say. "Out of that miscellaneous figure you've got to take into consideration: insurance; rehearsals; equipment hire; and new stage clothes, if you're so inclined." And just as he feels he's about to lose the tour he'll add, "Obviously, if you're on tour you'll sell truck loads of records so you'll be up on record royalties and publishing royalties. Then there's the swag. You've always been good for about ten grand a week on the swag, haven't you? And if the tickets sell well, there's always extra money to be earned as you'll break percentage every night."

In all seriousness, please always watch your bottom line and never ever pay to play, no matter what level you are on.

Just so that you can see how the £10,000 fee fits into the scheme of things, here's a semi-accurate breakdown of the kind of fees you can expect at the various venues:

The wee pub at the end of the road: Whatever you take on the door. Could be £10 and could even reach £100 if you have a great night.

The Pub Gigs on the circuit: Either a straight percentage of the door which could get you as much as £200 or a fee of £150.

The Jazz Café: Capacity 400,	£1,750.
Dingwall's Dance Hall: Cap. 500,	£2,500.
The Garage: Cap. 900,	£3,500+.
The Dominion Theatre: Cap. 1,900,	£4-£10,000.
Shepherd's Bush Empire: Cap. 2,000,	£5-£12,000.
Hammersmith Odeon: Cap. 3,400,	£10-£25,000.
The Royal Albert Hall: Cap. 5,600,	£8-£50,000.
Wembley Arena: Cap. 10,000,	£25-£100,000.
Wembley Stadium (RIP): Cap. 74,000,	£100-£350,000.
Reading or V Festivals: Cap. 50,000+,	£500,000+.
Knebworth: Cap. 200,000,	£1,000,000+.

The above guestimates are based on reasonable ticket price. For the Albert Hall I have shown the capacity as being 5,400, but the actual capacity the promoter and artist have access to is only 3,800. This is because when the venue was being built 1,600 people put money into the work. For this contribution they received a seat for life and they could either sell their seat on or pass it down to their heirs. It is the heirs who today receive the income from those seats. It's one of the most beautiful venues for an artist to play – I cannot think of a more magnificent stage to walk out onto. It's also a very artist- and audience-friendly venue.

Before we get bogged down in figures, let's just do one final costing here. This one is so that you can see how your fee comes out of the box-office gross of one of the above venues. Let's take Hammersmith Odeon. I know it's now called the Apollo but I can never get used to that after all the amazing Ry Cooder, Tom Waits, Jackson Browne, The Undertones, Little Village, John Lee Hooker, Christy Moore, Van Morrison, James Taylor, Crosby Stills and Nash shows we did in the Hammersmith Odeon days.

Costing For Hammersmith Odeon

Capacity: 3,400

Ticket Prices: £18.50, £16.50 & £14.50

Gross Potential:	£61,200
Nett Potential after VAT (Valued Added Tax):	£52,085.11

Running Costs:

Venue Rental:	£10,000.00	
Performing Rights Society (3%):	£1,562.55	
Follow spot – rental & operators:	£340.00	
Ticket Printing:	£200.00	
Stage Manager :	£200.00	
Advertising, poster printing and distribution:	£8,000.00	
Artwork :	£750.00	
Security:	£480.00	
Venue Crew:	£350.00	
Stage Crew:	£800.00	
First Aid & Fireman:	£70.00	
Catering:	£800.00	
Public Liability Insurance:	£99.00	
Non-appearance Insurance:	£360.00	
Production Phone:	£100.00	
Towels:	£14.40	
Taxis (venue crew):	£30.00	
Gratuities:	£80.00	
Total expenses:		£23,875.95
Nett after expenses (nett after VAT less expenses):		£28,209.05

This means if your act was on £10,000 against 85% nett, they will receive either a minimum of £10,000 or 85% of the nett whichever is the greater.

In our example above 85% of the nett is in fact £23,977.69. Which means the artist has more than doubled their guarantee, which kinda means that maybe the agent didn't pitch the fee as well as he, or she, should have. £20,000 would have been more on target.

So, on the above, the agent will receive 10% of the artist's fee, which works out at £2,399.

The promoter will receive £4,231.36 for his troubles. However, if the artist only sold half of the tickets, then the nett after VAT would only be £26,042.56. This means after his expenses, which would drop to approx £22,000, and the artists fee of £10,000, the promoter is going to lose £5,957.44. The artist would still receive his fee of £10,000 and the agent would still receive his commission of £1,000 and the promoter would go boo hoo hoo all the way home!

So, promoting is a risky business and if a Promoter loses badly on a night (as is the case with the above scenario) it will take them two or three good nights to make it back again – a bit like gambling, I suppose. A lot like gambling in fact.

But even gamblers like to minimise their risks, which brings to mind a development in the music business (particularly the business side of it) that you should be made aware of. In recent times, the concert side of the music business in the USA and UK has been under a darkening cloud of the SFX factor. Basically SFX are an American company who owned a few radio stations in America and started to buy up American Concert Promoters and American Concert Venues. They pretty much made a clean coast-to-coast sweep. With their new enlarged portfolio they went back to their investors and raised more funds. With these funds they started to repeat the process in Europe. They bought out the major promoters in Holland, Sweden, Denmark, Switzerland, Belgium and several promoters operating in England. Again, as in America, they bought several UK venues too. The most recent development is that they have bought three UK Agencies. All these deals were multimillion dollar deals. The problem I have with this situation is not where, in the market place, they are going to recoup their money but in all of this who is meant to be looking after the artists' interest?

You could, very easily, have a scenario in the UK where the one company will own your concert Promoter, your Agency and the venue you perform in. In that instance, I repeat my original question, who is going to be looking after the artist's interest? SFX have now sold out the whole caboodle to a company called Clear Channel. Now they are probably all very fine people who shake hands with old folks and kiss babies but you have to wonder where it will stop? Will they want to buy publishing companies? Record companies? Newspapers? Television stations? I think the fear we all live under is then they'll have the power to turn around and say to artists, "Here's the deal. It's the only deal in town. Like it or lump it." I'm sure I'm just being an alarmist and these fine people are all music fans who care not for dividends and share prices but only for the songs.

12. Time To Reflect And Think Of Managers

By now things are clicking into gear for Wire Crates. Say for the sake of our discussion the single caused a bit of a stir. It is given airtime on a few radio station play lists around the country. Maybe Mark Cooper, who books the talent for the *Later With Jools Holland* show, heard your CD, liked it and included you in one of Jools' television shows. That, plus your gigging, has created an audience for your debut album, which enters the chart in the top 20. You should be quite happy, but not ecstatic, with your progress to date. you're on target but only just. Things will start to become more complicated. Maybe now it's time to consider taking a manager. With your new profile you'll now find a different class of manager interested in you.

The likelihood is that there will be so much going on that you won't be able to keep on top of it. This is obviously the most vital point in your career to have a manager. Later, when you have broken through as an artist, a caretaker manager or PA (personal assistant) will suffice but right about the time of your first album charting you will have a platform and an opportunity from which to successfully launch your career. As well as building and consolidating your UK career you've got to consider other European territories. Experienced managers know how this system works; they know how to exploit it to your best advantage. Basically, the system necessitates climbing up on the bucking bronco and hanging on for dear life. If you are still seated when the bronco slows down you'll have done well.

After Europe, America, the most romantic of territories, will beckon. Historically it has to be stated that no matter how big a group/artist become in the UK/Mainland Europe if they don't break America they seldom last. Of course there are exceptions to every rule but I can't think of many. You might suggest Cliff Richard and then I'd say that Devil Woman was number six on the American charts. He also had two other American top 10 hits, so perhaps Cliff had America in his grasp and he chose to let it go, I really don't know. On top of this, few artists have had a European career to surpass Cliff's. Would Slade, T-Rex, Boyzone, Jam and all of the Brit Pop bands have split up if they'd conquered America? I think not. But the main point here is that if you've left your choice of management until now it's preferable to appoint a manager who has American experience. If that's not possible all is not lost. Simply appoint one who agrees to work with a co-manager in America.

In America, management is all about TCB – Taking Care of Business. It's all about follow-up. It's all about living on the phone. It's all about being on the case. With the time difference between Europe and America (New York City is five hours behind the UK and Los Angeles is a further three hours behind New York) it is nigh on impossible to do it successfully from the UK. Few have managed to accomplish this remarkable feat, whilst many have failed. Successful American managers leave nothing to chance. They won't be happy with you giving them four weeks of touring once a year. The only way to break America is to go over there regularly and work it. The reason Elvis Costello was the most successful of all the so-called UK punk acts was because Jake Riviera, his manager, knew the American way and their entire operation would decamp to America for six months at a time. But there are few Jakes around. Miles Copeland (Police & Sting) and Paul McGuinness (U2) spring to mind but the problem is they are no good for you and your act. You need to find a new Jake, a new Miles and a new Mr McGuinness. I think these are the three great managers of my generation. All have entirely different approaches and styles but all are totally motivated and artist driven.

In my career I have managed The Blues By Five, Fruupp, Radio Stars, Van Morrison (Business Arrangements was the exact title Van afforded me; Pee Wee Ellis did the Horn Arrangements for Van and I did the Business Arrangements), Gerry Rafferty, Dexy's Midnight Runners and Tanita Tikaram. With all of them, except Tanita, I was a caretaker manager. I started out as the agent – that's what I am, that's what I do, that's what I enjoy doing and that's what I'm proud to be. Tanita didn't have a manager at the time, so I was pulled in to take care of management duties.

Mostly I enjoyed the work. I resigned from Dexy's though after about a week. It was around the time of their *Don't Stand Me Down* album and pretty soon I realised that the only reason they wanted a manager was so as they would have someone around to say, "No!" to the record company on their behalf. All of the above artists were people whose music I loved and, just like the early days, someone was needed to help the artist put their show on the road. I try to avoid such a situation these days. I describe the role only to show you that at the juncture in Wire Crates' career that we are discussing (their first album threatening to take off big time) a caretaker manager is exactly what they don't need. They should hold out until they find the right person and, as I say, with help from your lawyer, your accountant and your agent, you will find someone. Again I've included a few names at the back but I would remind you that when you are interviewing anyone it is of vital importance that you are their number one act. No matter how much you may appear to like the manager's presentation and pitch, if they are managing several other acts at the same time remove them from your shortlist immediately.

13. The Firsts

The first time things happen to you in this business is quite exciting and exhilarating. I think it's exactly the same feeling whether you're the artist, the agent or the manager. You know, milestone events like the excitement of your first mention in *Melody Maker* (RIP, but they did help to dig their own grave). In most instances your first mention would be in the classified section and a single-column wide, four cm deep and it would have said something like 'WIRE CRATES – semi-pro band with org. material need drummer. No wasters need apply. Ring Tony on Whitehall 1212.' Yep small, insignificant and nobody probably even noticed it except you and the people you tipped off. Drummers always seemed to be the hardest to get. It might be because most of them play with several groups, giving up on six when the seventh takes off.

Your next first will be when you see your name appear advertising your gig. Again, returning to the halcyon *Melody Maker* days, this usually meant you were opening for Brewers Droop at the Nag's Head in High Wycombe but it didn't matter, you were in the club pages. The club pages were vitally important. So many times when you rang up to get a gig, the venue bookers or managers would use the *Melody Maker* and *NME* club pages as their *Bible*. The more appearances you had the more likely you were going to get a booking. The more bookings you got the more you were in the club pages… the more you were in the club pages… I'm sure you get the picture.

Thin Lizzy (or Tin Lizzie if you misheard their accents) worked out a very good short cut for this circuit. They went to several venues who maybe ran on a Friday and Saturday only and persuaded the promoters to give them one of the other five free nights with no guarantee, just a straight percentage of the door receipts. Then, having amassed twenty or so gigs they persuaded their record company to place small adverts in the club section of *Melody Maker* and *NME* in the style of the venue's own ads and pumped away at this, week after week. Pretty soon, both the club owners and, more importantly, the audiences wanted to see what this group was all about. Then they released 'Whiskey In The Jar' and the rest is history, some of it happy some of it sad.

In the clubs – places like The 76 Club in Burton-upon-Trent, the 1832 Club in Windsor, The Foxx at Croydon, Heads in Wimbledon, The Red Lion in Leytonstone – the rule of thumb was that you would play about three times as a support act and then you'd get an opportunity to headline. Headlining was a major first. Of course, we're talking here about a time when there was a healthy club circuit. Getting your first encore was the next major first, only this one was one with knobs on. This is usually followed with your first write-up, usually in a local paper where you'd be mentioned in the main act's review: 'Wire Crates entertained the packed house until local sensation Brewer's Droop took the stage and worked everyone up into a frenzy blah, blah, blah…'

But at least you'd got your first mention, which is better than being ignored. Well maybe not. Once people start to pay attention to you they start to listen to you and (sometimes) that's when you wished that the press were still ignoring you: 'With sloppy playing and pretentious material, Wire Crates better watch themselves or they'll soon be in dire straits. Main act Fruupp however wooed the crowd with their magical material.' That's not a quote from the *Fishmongers' Gazette* in Grimsby but it could have been.

You proceed through your firsts. First photo in the paper. First blowing-off of the main act. First write-up. First encounter with a groupie (always after your first write-up, never before). First record deal. First record session. First record sleeve. First play on the radio (usually Radio Caroline at 3.20 a.m. and you only hear half of the song because the weak signal keeps washing in and out, but you and the rest of their audience – seagulls – really enjoy it). First play on Radio One. And then your wildest dream come true – your first chart entry. Hallelujah! It's a big one this so I'll shout that again. Hallelujah!

Assuming your record company has been doing their work to ensure each and every chart shop (there are lists available) in the country has several copies of your single (mostly freebies) and a wee bit of a buzz starting and people are starting to go into the shops and ask for, "Wire Crates' new single, The Essential Song" and maybe even some of them (like your families) will buy more than one copy and the following Monday morning you hear that your single sold 457 copies and entered the chart at number 98. Jubilation, celebrations!! I really can't describe to you the joy that you will feel achieving this wondrous milestone. You will feel such a rush you will literally be walking on air. You won't be able to sleep because you will be so consumed by the fact that you've got your first single in the charts.

The following week the single climbs to 79. Your single has legs! The record company proceeds to do a bit of creative marketing – giving away more freebies to the chart return shops – and the following week your single drops to 80. Oops! Misery, your first flop! But maybe not. The following week it climbs to 67. So it's back on track. Then the week after it jumps to number 42, missing the national chart (the top 40) by just two places. The following week the record company goes out to do its work, your family, friends and relations go out and buy several more copies each, your enemies return complimentary copies to the record stores. Now because you're a new act and bubbling under the charts you will start to receive a certain amount of media attention. Here it will help greatly if you have a press hook that your PR person can work on. You know, the sort of things that set you apart from the rest of the field. Things like the lead singer having a famous girlfriend (highly unlikely because you're not famous enough yet yourself), or one of the members of the band being related to someone like Edwina Curry (she seems to love media attention, so she'll be good for any available photo opportunity).

You'll be dreading and loving that Sunday Radio One Countdown show. When the DJ plays the number 40 record, you'll think, "Great, at least we didn't just make the forty." This thought will continue until he gets to, say, the number 32 chart entry. Then you'll start to think, "Shit, we didn't make the top 40 at all!" By the time the DJ gets to 30 you'll feel absolutely terrible. You'll be exhausted, wrecked, drained and you'll wonder why because all you have been doing is listening to the radio. But the problem is that every second of the week you have just gone through will have been spent concentrating on the countdown and now it's all over. You'll kick yourself for not doing that extra round of the special chart return shops in your area. (Check out *I Love The Sound of Breaking Glass* for more on the art of chart hyping.) The masochist in you will force you to continue listening to the radio and then you'll hear at number 29 the song that you hate by a group you know and last week their single was at 47 and here it is! That is why you will hate the song. You'll hate them and their song in equal portions because you'll feel that they have stolen your opportunity.

You'd like to take the radio and shove it through the window but you can't because all your family is sitting around you and they have all started to grow embarrassed by your failure to reach the charts. Your mother has probably already mentally spent her share of the royalties on a new suite of furniture for the living room. What share of royalties? Oh yes she was going to speak to you about that at the appropriate moment. You'll be so mad that you probably won't hear the DJ announce, "And at 28, yet another new entry from a new group, this time it's Wire Crates and The Essential Song." Someone in the room will let out an embarrassing howl and there'll be several shouts and yelps but no matter how great the excitement it will all sound a wee bit stifled, a wee bit stiff. The Americans are much better at this kind of stuff than we are. They are so much more uninhibited publicly than we are. Just look at the audiences in their game shows compared to ours. But the celebrations will continue around you. You'll be in a daze. Then you'll realise exactly what all the fuss was about when you hear the opening bars to your song being played on the national radio as the official number 28 best-selling song in the country. It's a legit hit and things will never ever be the same again. Savour these precious moments. From now on every time this current single, and all future singles, moves up the pop charts you'll feel okay, just okay. If it drops however, you'll feel totally gutted. Why then, if it feels so terrible if the single drops, does it not feel proportionally better when it moves up the chart? I don't know. All I can tell you is that it doesn't. And it's growing even more difficult in the current climate where the record company's rule of thumb is: if you don't make the top 40 in the first week you are not going to make the top 40. So, in some instances, it's all over in a week and you can't imagine how bad you are going to feel if that happens.

But the excitement we're talking about on your first hit is pretty much unbeatable, unless of course you achieve another first and your single takes over the coveted number one spot. Now that's an entirely different story altogether.

14. Ferry Across The Atlantic & Other Short Stories

When you become famous people start to tell stories about you. Some of the stories will be true, some start with a grain of truth, but by the time they've been passed around a few road crews the original story will have become seriously embellished. For instance, a certain 1960s pop star (not one of the artists I represent, I hasten to add) spent so much of his time on the road continuously touring that he pretty much lived in Holiday Inn Hotels. When he did take a break from touring for long enough to buy himself his first flat, all his mates were shocked to see he'd decorated his flat entirely in the style of Holiday Inn. Now the truth in that story was probably that he simply hung a lamp, by chain, from the ceiling over his dining table in the corner of the room à la Holiday Inn but I'm sure you'll agree that doesn't quite have the same impact as the roadie version.

Artists sometimes do tend to lose it; but on the other hand we seem to expect nothing less from them. Elton John famously rang up his management office one day to complain about the wind blowing noisily outside his window and demanding they do something about it.

Talking about photographs (which we weren't) reminds me of another wee tale I'd like to share with you. A manager I know, a star manager in fact, had just recently taken on Brian Ferry. Mr Ferry, as we all know, is quite a looker and by all accounts he's quite proud of his looks. Mr Ferry was due to fly to America for several days' promotion. Cars were organised and our star manager was probably looking forward to a few artist-free days when he got a call from the record company saying that the driver of the car that had been sent around to collect Mr Ferry couldn't raise an answer at the door and they were in danger of missing the flight.

The manager got the artist on the phone. The manager asked what the problem was. The artist replied that he would be unable to go to America because he didn't have a passport. But of course Mr Ferry had a passport the manager protested. Sure, hadn't his office gone to the trouble of organising the whole procedure, filling in forms, collating all the necessary documents, depositing them at the passport office and then a few days later collecting the official passport from the passport office and delivering it to Mr Ferry's very own house.

Mr Ferry persisted with the story that he didn't have a passport. When the manager eventually proved that the passport had been sent to the house, Mr Ferry relented somewhat and admitted that he had in fact received the passport but that he didn't have it in his possession any more.

"Why," the manager asked close to the edge, "What happened to it?"

"I tore it up and threw it in the dustbin?" the artist replied.

"What? Why on earth did you do that?" the exasperated manager continued.

"Oh, I didn't like the photograph you used."

Moving (very) swiftly along.

As you can see, I enjoy quite a wide variety of music but it seems to me that there has always been a Don Williams muse in my life. You know what I mean, don't you? We're talking here about someone with a deep brown voice that sings predominantly autumn music. Before Don Williams, it would have been Jim Reeves and after Don it would have been Randy Travis. I particularly like Don Williams singing the songs of Bob McDill (another of my favourite songwriters). McDill is a great man for fitting little stories into songs and I've often thought that the following Don Williams story might just be a basis for such a song.

Don Williams was touring Europe with a tour manager friend of mine. It was the first time this particular tour manager had worked with Mr Williams and he was anxious to get everything right for the artist. On one particular occasion the entourage had just checked into their hotel in yet another European capital. The tour manager, check-in operation safely executed, was enjoying a well-earned respite rummaging through the mini bar and the movie channels, when he received a telephone call from Mr Williams summoning him to the artist's suite post-haste to sort out a major problem.

A few minutes later a flush-faced tour manager entered Don Williams' room. He quickly glanced around the room looking for the offending conundrum. Mr Williams was reclining nonplussed on the bed, his trademark cowboy hat and cowboy boots very evident. The tour manager looked around the room unable to find anything wrong. The problem, Mr Williams eventually disclosed, was that he couldn't see his television properly from his current position on the bed. On close inspection the tour manager worked out that the television was obscured only by the artist's famous large boots. The tour manager suggested that Mr Williams move his feet just a matter of ten inches to the left.

"Nope, they're perfectly fine where they are, Sir," came the reply in the slow Southern drawl, "Why don't you just move the television ten inches to the right."

All together now, "You're my friend..."

But not all of the good tales are road ones. Now and again the office produces some of its own. My partner and co-owner of Asgard, Paul Fenn, once took on Joe Fagin who had a number three hit with 'That's Livin' Alright,' the signature tune for *Auf Wiedersehen, Pet*. One morning, he received a very attractive faxed offer for Mr Fagin to visit The United Emirates. Mr Fagin and his manager immediately accepted the offer and the concert was confirmed. Some time later, before the concert, Paul received another fax from the promoter wanting to know did Mr Fagin still perform 'Rickie Don't Lose That Number.' It soon became clear that the promoter had mistaken his Mr Fagens. He thought he was booking the Mr Donald Fagen – whose turn (band) Steely Dan had indeed recorded and released a hit called 'Rickie Don't Lose That Number' – and not the Mr Joe Fagin we represented.

And, sticking with the office, then there's the Subcircus story. Subcircus are one of our new groups agented by Mick Griffiths – the essential name on the agents' list at the back of the book. The band were booked for a tour and Mick's PA was in the office late one night busy on the phones collating the details for their itinerary – the tour *Bible* which contains all the essentials for the band's tour dates, venues, hotels addresses, telephone numbers, times, etc. Mick's PA rang up one of the gigs, and she asked the gentleman who answered the phone for the address. He gave her the address and no one thought any more about it until several weeks later when the band and their truck and their tour bus turned up at a housing site in Derby. It turns out that the chap who answered the phone call asking for the address was in fact the club bar man and he had quite innocently given his home address. The home address in question was a simple two up and two down house and several frantic phone calls later the mistake was discovered. All's well that ends well – 30 minutes or so later the band's amused crew were setting up their equipment in the club.

Some strange requests for Van Morrison used to come into the office. I remember receiving a very polite letters from Van's major fans. One particular fan, from the west country, was due to be married and had written in seeking permission to use music from Van's masterpiece *Astral Weeks* at the church service. The letter included all the details of the wedding, the church and the pieces of music they wished to use. I passed the request on to Van who approved the use and I duly passed Van's approval on to the happy couple. I didn't think any more of the matter until a few weeks later I received a telephone call from the newlyweds. The groom was gushing on the phone and he was so excited that at first I couldn't pick up what he was trying to say. Eventually I managed to ascertain that Van Morrison had not only turned up in person at the wedding the previous weekend but he'd even gone as far as singing a few selections at the church service. The bride and groom were still beside themselves with joy a few days later and who could blame them. I mention the tale to conclude this chapter only to show that the pictures of artists that are painted by the press are not always the kinder ones.

15. The Dream Team

Let's talk a bit now about putting your dream team together.

I suppose that like most other sections of the entertainment industry, the music business is littered with artists who never really quite made it and still don't know how to give up. You put anyone on a stage, somewhere, anywhere, and someone will turn up to watch and listen to the performer. And this is all the encouragement most of the aforementioned artists need to continue. They are prepared to sacrifice their wealth, their health and their heart in order to be allowed to bask in the spotlight. Be that the light from a 60-watt bulb at the Half Moon, Putney, or, from 20 Super trooper spotlights at Wembley Arena.

These artists and their entourages – musicians, managers, agents, roadies, parents, wives, boyfriends, girlfriends, lawyers, accountants – continually intrigue me, and I've been working in this area for 30 years now. Why do they keep going? Why do they never achieve the success of some of their contemporaries? Some certainly have a body of work deserving greater success. I'm equally intrigued by how musicians come together to form a band, and how the hierarchy of the band is decided in the first few months of the band's life. For instance if Brian Jones hadn't lost out in the power struggle with Andrew Loog Oldham in the Rolling Stones wars then perhaps they'd be more of a Chicken Skin Music type of band than the Grandfather of Rock they've become.

In one of my crime novels, *The Ballad Of Sean And Wilko*, I really enjoyed putting together my own fictional group, Circles, and surrounding them, with a team of characters but even my fictitious dream team will never be as unpredictable as your real team.

In the all-important first few months of putting your group together you'll note the initial shuffling of feet as your co-members jockey for position. Again, potentially, these are the people whose pocket you are going to live in for at least the next 5 or so years and maybe even as much as the following 2 or 3 decades. So my advice is to observe your colleagues closely and if you need to replace troublesome members, do it immediately. It will be much easier than waiting a few years when they're sharing the spotlight with you. The infamous firing of Pete Best nearly derailed The Beatles from their mega-successful path.

One of the guys in Fruupp liked to drink a bit too much. He was a sweetheart when sober but a right royal pain in the posterior when he had a few on him. What I'm saying is that we, the other musicians and myself, might have saved ourselves a lot of anguish and frustration if we had parted company in the very early days. Who knows? We might even have been more successful. Hey, but you can't live your life on might-have-beens. If Fruupp had been successful then I might have been in a position where I would not have been able, and continued to be able, to work with a lot of great artists.

Apart from which, not all drinkers are bad people. I remember a story from the days when I worked with Northern Irish & Scottish traditional group, The Boys Of The Lough. Cathal McConnell can sing through his flute sweeter and more soulfully than anyone else on this earth. As you know, blowing air into an instrument is thirsty work. Anyway, on one memorable occasion he'd gone from the gig to a pub with his mates and then, after a few jars in the pub, back to one of his mates' houses for a drinking session. The Boys Of The Lough were scheduled to leave first thing the following morning to catch a flight so Cathal knew that no matter what happened, no matter what state he was in or got into, he had to get back to the group hotel. So in the early hours of the morning he left his mates, still in full flow, and made his way back in the direction of the hotel. A few wrong turns later he stumbled into the lobby of a hotel only to discover that he'd lost his key. At least he'd his precious flute with him so he spent a few minutes waking up the hotel receptionist who, still half sleeping, took Cathal up to the second floor. Cathal thought he must be a lot drunker than he first realised because he was sure that the receptionist was letting him into a room on the opposite side of the corridor.

Cathal was so wrecked by the time he got into the room he fell straight into the bed. Do you know where this is going? Yep, you've got it. There was already someone in his bed. Actually it wasn't Cathal's bed; it wasn't even Cathal's hotel. No, his hotel was next door. The couple already occupying the bed was, as you can imagine, shocked to say the least, but not Cathal. Without missing a beat he snuggled up even closer to the female and said, "Ah, sure now that I'm here I may as well stay."

I can't tell you what happened next. All I'll say is that it was another adventure in The Boys Of The Lough story where alcohol added to the fun that kept them going. As I mentioned earlier, this isn't always the case and in lots of heavily-documented instances alcohol and drugs have brought many an artist to a premature and expensive end. Yes, fun is fun and we all enjoy our personal indulgences but there is a time and a place and, I'm sure, a limit on available funds.

There's the story that George Jones once received an advance of $100,000 from a record company. This is a lot of money these days but in those days it was an absolute fortune. Allegedly, or so the quote goes, Mr Jones spent the majority of the advance on cocaine – the rest he completely wasted.

When you're putting your band together, choose your fellow travellers wisely. That's all I'm saying. To some degree it's easier if you want to be a solo artist. You can hire and fire your musicians as you need them.

The other issue, which needs to be brought to your attention at this stage, is how your income is to be divided up. Again if you are a solo act, at least on paper, it's pretty simple. You write the songs, you hire musicians to help you perform and record them so you receive all the money, right? It's not always as simple as that.

Say you write a song, a great song for the sake of this discussion, and you go into the studio with a bunch of musicians to record your masterpiece. During the recording, the saxophone player comes up with this amazing head-turning intro(duction) to the recording of your song, or the guitarist plays a classic guitar solo to fill the gap in the middle of your song. Nothing more is thought of it until the record comes out and begins to storm its way up the charts all over the world. The money starts to roll in. That's when the trouble starts. You see, when a hired musician plays on a record he or she receives a flat (Musicians Union approved) payment. It doesn't (in theory) matter to him, or her, if the record sells ten copies to your family members or ten million copies to a growing army of fans worldwide. However, the closer the figure is to ten million the higher the chances that, all of a sudden, the saxophone player will claim he wrote the intro and that it's the intro that is the hook and the reason that the song is such a hit and, wait for it, yes, the reason he should receive some of the publishing royalties. The guitarist will chip into the discussion that, "Well really it's not much of a song if you take the guitar solo out and hey I'm due a share of the royalties, too."

The simple solution is to have the musicians sign a receipt when they are being paid for their recording services saying, "For full and final payment." Equally, if you should happen to be either the saxophone player or guitar player in the above situation, deal with it immediately. If you come up with an original contribution to the song, make your feelings known immediately and if you can't come to an agreement advise them that you'd prefer that your work be removed from the track.

Sting was invited by Mark Knopfler to come down to the studio to sing guest vocals on one of Dire Straits' records. Sting's contribution to the song was so distinctively Sting that, near enough on the spot, Mark gave him a co-writer credit and a share of the publishing on the song. The song was 'Money For Nothing' and the situation was dealt with correctly and professionally so all concerned were perfectly pleased when it became the worldwide smash hit it did.

In a band set-up, it's never quite as simple as that. For instance, even though you have a band where all members are equal partners, you will still have someone who writes the majority, if not all, of the material. So you all slog around the country for years trying to make ends meet, preaching the gospel according to the writer's songs and building up an audience. The audience arrives and the albums start to sell and then, suddenly, one in your midst (the songwriter) starts to receive a lot more money than the rest of you and it's hard to feel equal at that stage. He moves into a mansion in Hampstead while you purchase a flat in Camden Town. He drives around in a Jaguar S Type while you have to make do with your Fiat Punto. No mater how good a mate he once was, no matter how aware you are that he writes all the songs, you're still going to feel pissed off and you feeling pissed off can be the fatal crack in the dyke.

On the other hand, if you give your non-songwriting fellow band members a piece of your songs, eventually you are going to resent them, particularly if and when the band splits up and they are still receiving a percentage of your songs.

How do you get over this particular sharp spiked hurdle?

The Beatles got over it by giving George and Ringo a percentage of their publishing company, Northern Songs. George eventually started to come up with a Northern Song or two of his own and classics they were too. For other solutions check what other bands do by looking at the songwriting credits on album sleeves. The Doors, Rockpile and U2 for example make for interesting reading.

There is just one further bit of advice I'd like to give you before we move away from the songwriting side of things. When, and if, you have your first hit, you are going to be totally gobsmacked by the number of people who will come out of the woodwork. I have to tell you that there are some sorry and sad people out there who will convince themselves and others that they have written your hit songs. I'm sure you've witnessed some very famous cases in the press. Now of course we all know that you are the songwriter and the song comes from your pen and your pen alone, but a judge is not going to simply take your word for it. You are going to have to take time out of your busy schedule and employ a legal team to address this issue. So, my tip is, each and every time you write a song record it onto a cassette, place the cassette in an envelope with a hand-written copy of the lyrics including any changes and any wee notes or documents, which might show where you got the ideas for your song. Seal the package, write on the outside of the envelope the title(s) of the song(s) included and send it to yourself by registered post. This process will date and time your work. When you receive the package in the post, don't break the seal, file it away carefully for some point in the future when it just might come in handy for you.

There are also other political issues surrounding the band involving boyfriends, girlfriends, mothers, fathers, husbands, wives and even cheating amongst all of the above. For greater details on this I'd suggest you check out *The Ballad Of Sean And Wilko*. But before you start to think, 'Goodness, do I really want to bother with the music business at all?' let's press on with our team.

The Dream Team

Managers: We've dealt with them, so strike them off your list.

Lawyers and/or Solicitors: Obviously they are needed to protect you legally and to ensure, along with your accountant, that all your business is in order. They charge by the hour anything from £100 per hour for assistants and £250 to £400 an hour for partners. But in each project they do for you get an estimate in advance – never wait for an invoice to arrive to see what your legal bills are. They will deal with the legal issue in your contracts with record companies, managers, agents, music publishers, merchandisers and sponsors. You must still, however, heavily involve yourself in all these and other issues of your contracts particularly the artistic matters.

Accountants: See also details for Lawyers above. Your accountants will also be responsible for giving you advice on tax matters, VAT matters, on auditing your various royalty statements and, occasionally, helping you to protect your money long-term. An accountant will charge you in the region of £50 an hour. I would recommend that you do not permit your accountant or lawyers to set up a series of complicated companies to handle your income. Keep it simple; keep it very simple. That way it's very easy for you to keep on top of it. In all the deals you do with people who will pay you money (record companies, concert promoters, publishing companies, merchandising companies etc.) have the contracts worded so that all funds go directly to you and to no one else. You can then, in turn, pay the invoices of those who provide you with a service. Always sign your own cheques. That is so important; important enough for me to mention again. Always have all your income paid directly to you. Always pay your own bills. Always sign your own cheques.

The Tour Manager: Worth his or her weight in gold. Basically a really good tour manager will help you and your manager co-ordinate the live side of your career. Some develop into either artist's PA, or manager's PA, or manager's partner, or co-manager. A few even end up as the managers themselves. But in the initial stages they will take on only the responsibilities of the roadwork. You can find a tour manager by either promoting someone already in your road crew or by hiring one of the freelancers. There are lots around and your agent will know and work with the best and the worst of them and will, hopefully, tip you off accordingly. They charge anything from £500 to £3,000 per week while you're touring. If you require one exclusively, i.e. they work with you and only you, you will also have to pay them a retainer during the time you are not on the road.

The Publicist: Is responsible for your press coverage or lack of it. Van Morrison once hired a publicist to keep him out of the press – or so the publicist claimed. They are either employees of the record company who work on you around the time your records are released, or you hire your own to look after you annually. The same goes for finding your PR firm as goes for finding your agent. Don't go with someone just because their firm also represents David Bowie or Paul McCartney. Go with someone you feel knows what you are trying to do with your music and someone you feel understands you. Make sure you are comfortable chatting to them. Independent PR companies will charge whatever they can get, say around £1,200 to £10,000 per month.

The Record Plugger: The person responsible for getting you and your music on radio and television. An important thing to remember though is that, according to your plugger, if your song gets on the radio, it's because your plugger did a great job and if your song doesn't get on the radio, it's because you've written a crap song. I've actually sat in a meeting at East West Records where the radio pluggers said, about a new Tanita Tikaram single, that the radio stations didn't want to play a particular song because it was too slow, "It's a ballad," he said, "they want Tanita Tikaram to do something different," he said. Tanita's next single was in fact an upbeat song. The same plugger reported, "They (Radio Onederful) won't play this," he said. "This is not what they expect from her. They want a great big slow ballad from Tanita Tikaram." I kid you not. That's what he said. Basically you can't let it worry you. Radio stations play what they want to play and your plugger is only the messenger – to them with the music and to you with the bad news. As with the publicist, some are record company employees or, if you wish to hire your own they charge pretty much the same as the PR firms.

The Record Company: We've discussed them already quite a bit but maybe a quote from Robin Blanchflower (an A& R guy for a large record company) sums it all up as well as I could. He was sending a rejection letter to the manager of the group Japan, 'This group has a lot of potential,' he wrote. 'Unfortunately we are not in the potential business.' Worth noting here I suppose that this was the same Robin Blanchflower who signed Fruupp to the label he was working with, at that time, Pye Records. We were happy to go there just because they had been the home of The Kinks. Wrong reason!

The Publishing Company: We've also discussed them and I include a few names at the back of the book.

The Merchandising Company: Sign with the merchandising company who will pay you the most money in advance and who won't ask for some or all of it back again when you don't sell the volume they expect you to. At the same time, allow them only to produce items you would be happy to use yourself. Make sure you write lots of freebies into your contract.

Record Producers: Again a very, very personal choice and it's probably wise to vary them from record to record. I know you're not meant to change a winning team but then you also have to consider the boredom factor. For producers, I've included the names of a few people who look after producers just to give you a wide selection but don't forget Malcolm will have record producers names dripping out of his ears.

Road Crews: Definitely the people who not only keep the show on the road but the wheels on the vehicles. Again, it's invaluable to you if at least a couple of them can work with you the whole way through your career. It means you're going to have a solid foundation to your crew. Most of the road crews I've worked with are loyal to a fault to their artists. One of the tour manager's roles is to help you put the road crew together. How much do road crews get paid? Never enough, so always pay them what you can afford to pay them.

In picking your team, trust is a word that is often used and it is a great quality to find in someone, but for their sake as well as your own, never put anyone in the position where you are wondering whether or not you can actually trust them. So, set your business up so that the word trust doesn't come into it. It's pretty simple. I've mentioned it before but it certainly is important enough to bring to your attention again – word all of your contracts so that all income owed to you is paid directly to you or your wholly owned company, then you in turn pay the people who provide you with a service.

That's it, that's your dream team in place. That was easy wasn't it?

Maybe yes, maybe no. To a certain degree it's down to a wee bit of luck and a lot to do with great songs. In all of this, it doesn't really matter how good your dream team are, if you haven't got the songs. If it comes from the songs you've got a chance. If you sit at home thinking, 'The Music Business – that's a glamorous business, lots of girls/boys, lots of drugs, lots of booze and lots of dosh, yes I'll have a bit of that.' Then if I were you, I'd think again.

On the other hand, if you have things to say that you are desperate to say, and songs that you just must write and perform, then lock that bedroom door from the inside, start getting those songs down immediately and prepare yourself for the journey of a lifetime.

If you've done all of the above, followed it to the letter, and you still haven't succeeded don't come asking for a refund. All is not yet lost because as they say in the music business, "If at first you don't succeed then move to Ireland." It worked big time for Chris Rea and David Gray

And if you're a boy band or a girl band or a combo band (boys and girls), and you've got this far then I would suggest you ring Louis Walsh in Dublin, no one does it better than him.

16. The Root Of The Audience

I've been doing this one way or another now for 30 plus years and I still don't fully understand the genesis of an audience – your audience; any audience. You put your tickets on sale – it might be for a pub, which holds a hundred or so people, or it might be for Michael Jackson's record-breaking 7-night run at Wembley Stadium a few years back – and a certain amount of people buy tickets and turn up for the event. The same applies to sports, the cinema and the theatre. People just turn up. Why do they turn up? Why, sometimes, do they decide not to turn up?

The closest comparison I can come up with is the process you go through when you are lighting a fire.

You can have your fireplace packed perfectly with newspaper twists, twigs, small sticks, larger sticks, logs, coal and more logs. If you set it all up properly all you have to do is light the corner of one of the paper twists with a match and whoosh! your fire has taken and your hearth is filled with cheek-flushing flames. My dad's an expert at it. All he needs is a little paper, a few bits of wood and coal and he can get it going immediately and every single time. The same goes for my wife Catherine. She just sets up her system and it works every time. I, on the other hand, can have all of the above and even cheat a bit with firelighters, not to mention (sometimes) an entire box of matches, but it doesn't matter how much I huff and puff, I still won't be able to create a fire.

So you can see why I sometimes think that the creation of an audience is somewhat similar. You can have all of your set-up perfectly in place with posters, adverts, leaflets, newspaper stories, radio plugs, television plugs and a mention on the artist's Website. Then you try to ignite the fire by putting the tickets on sale and… no whoosh! The main difference between the making a fire and making an audience is that there is a secret to lighting a fire. Catherine and my father know this secret. In the music business though, no one has the secret of setting the audience on fire.

I've hung around many a venue entrance hall, marvelling at people as they turn up in twos and threes and sometimes even solo. That is, if they turn up at all. There is a horrible feeling of emptiness in the pit of your stomach at the thought that no one is going to come along at all to see your artist. Then they start to arrive in dribs and drabs and the relief you feel is akin to getting the all clear from your dentist while lying petrified in his chair – I know of no greater relief. The doors open at, say, 7 p.m. and the artist is meant to go on at 8 p.m. The audience will trickle in, the last one miraculously taking their seat just as the house lights dim.

I often hang around the lobby of the venue during this period. I am still so in awe of an audience as a body showing up. Sometimes you have an opportunity to use this time effectively by giving out flyers for your other forthcoming shows, a practice known as leafleting. You can learn so much from an audience during this time. I remember once I was handing out leaflets at a BB King concert at Hammersmith Odeon. The concert wasn't one of ours but it was the perfect target audience for a forthcoming concert we were promoting in the same venue with the Robert Cray Band. We were taking a major step up with Robert. His previous concert had been in the Electric Ballroom in Camden Town, which is about half of the capacity of the Hammersmith Odeon but we felt it would work. The Robert Cray Band was on the rise. There was a bit of a buzz around him. He had a sweet Sam Cooke kinda voice, played guitar like a veteran and he looked cool. He was just maybe a wee bit too young and good looking to take up his position amongst the blues greats at that point. Anyway, we'd spent quite a bit of money on advertising the concert. We'd taken our adverts in the usual papers: *The Sunday Times*; *The Evening Standard*; *Time Out*; and *NME*. We'd printed and distributed our posters. Now although the tickets were selling okay they weren't exactly flying out the door and I was shocked to find as I handed out the leaflets that people were finding out about the show for the first time. There was genuine surprise and interest generated from the BB King punters. You see, sometimes you take your expensive adverts and print and distribute your beautiful posters and no one notices. No one that is, except for the artist, the manager, the agent and the promoter. Real humans buy their papers and they don't stop at every advert and take in all the details. Mostly they pass by the adverts without a glance. But you stick a leaflet in the hand of a blues fan on their way into a venue to see BB King and there is a good chance they will want to buy a ticket for Robert Cray. And that is exactly what happened. The BB King audience went out over the next few weeks and bought their Robert Cray Band tickets and then, when you have a couple of thousand people walking around with Robert Cray Band tickets in their wallets, that is the best advert you can get. They talk to their mates about it and pretty soon those 2,000 tickets become 2,500 tickets and very soon you've sold out at 3,400 tickets. Tickets were sold and Robert Cray did the rest, it was a magic concert.

When the audiences don't appear, agents and promoters, have a long list of reasons to offer artists and managers.

- It's school and college exam time.
- It's school and college holiday time.
- So and so were here last night.
- So and so are here tomorrow night.
- There's been a non-stop run of concerts and the market place is saturated.
- People were expecting a bus/tube/train strike.
- There was a bus/tube/train strike.
- The ticket price might have been just a wee bit too high.
- The ticket price might have been just a wee bit too cheap.
- The promoter is just back from holiday.
- The single was late.
- The single was too early. People have already forgotten about it.
- There is never an excuse number 13. It's too much like bad luck.
- The album hasn't come out yet and people like to familiarise themselves with the new music before they come and see you live.
- Music is no longer the priority it once was in young people's lives.
- Either Inspector Morse or Inspector Christy Kennedy is on television tonight.
- Kids spend all their time surfing the net these days.

And on and on you can go and yes, some of them will be valid reasons but yet at the same time, Oasis can put two shows at Knebworth (400,000 give or take a hundred thousand) in the middle of exams in the middle of a tube and train strike and they'll make one announcement and before they get a chance to advertise it properly both shows will be sold out with twice the number of requests for tickets as are available.

Why do we listen to music in the first place? For enjoyment, I suppose. For comfort. For companionship. To have a soundtrack for your thoughts. To have a special place you know you can return to each and every time you put on a particular piece of music. How do audiences decide what music they like and which artists they are going to go and see and hear? The reality is, we probably start subconsciously by enjoying the music our parents or our older siblings are listening to. Then just as we turn 10 or 11, we start to show some form of independence and go off to explore our own tastes or tune in to what our schoolmates are listening to. Then we hear something we like with a passion and the whole aspect of the live performance of it intrigues us. Before records, music was kept alive by live performances but if the sales figures are anything to go by, live music is more popular than ever. So we've left the original reason far behind and replaced it with a more social one. It's a form of meeting and social interaction. Audiences, separated by neither language, colour nor religion come together to enjoy music being made.

So, where does Wire Crates' audience come from? If, on your way to the top, you play Hammersmith Odeon (3,400 capacity) and sell it out, does this mean that someone else (Michael Bolton for instance) has lost 3,400 members of his audience? The truth is that you share your audience with several artists. Long gone are the days when you could only like either The Beatles or The Rolling Stones. Assuming audiences are shared, how is your audience made up? It would be very easy if we were able to compartmentalise them – for example, if you like The Beatles you will also like A, B & C but if you like the Rolling Stones then you will like X, Y & Z.

I love the music of Bob Dylan but I don't particularly like what Michael Bolton does. Sadly, however, I am sure there are people who like Bob Dylan who also love Michael Bolton's work. I know, I know but you tell me why? I've never been able to figure it out.

You see, when it comes to audiences, none of us really know who they are or where they come from. Why will they decide to go and see their favourite artist one night and thoroughly enjoy the evening, yet the next time the same artist is on tour they will vote with their feet by staying away?

For my part, when I go to a magic show (Van Morrison at the Rainbow Theatre in London; Rockpile at Loughborough University; The Blue Nile at The Dominion Theatre in London; The Kinks at The Bilzen Festival; Jackson Browne at Palladium in New York or Genesis (with Peter Gabriel) at The Alexandra Theatre in Birmingham), I am so moved I have trouble putting my feelings into words. At all of the above concerts I could feel the hairs on the back of my neck stand up, I could feel tears welling up and I couldn't have talked to anyone even if I'd wanted to.

I was moved by the power of the music.

I count myself to be very lucky, not to say privileged, to have been present on those six occasions and to have witnessed what were, for me, the perfect shows. But I bet you that on the six nights I am talking about, there were people in the audience who were not as spellbound by the music as much as I was. You know, I am sure there were people there only because their boyfriends, girlfriends, wives or husbands insisted they be there or persuaded them to be there. It's a bit like the great story Ned Sherrin tells about an empty seat at a hit show in theatreland.

The story goes that during an incredible run of a fabulously successfully show – you know, sold out for years, tickets like gold dust – the theatre manager was doing his pre-curtain-up check of the audience. To his horror he discovered an empty seat. He checked with the box-office manager who confirmed that every seat in the house had been sold and paid for. When theatres post their 'house full' signs they like the theatre to be truly full. So the manager goes to the lady sitting next to the empty seat and asks does she know whom the seat belongs to. She told the manager it belonged to her husband. He couldn't be there but she was so looking forward to the amazing show she came by herself anyway.

"But does he realise what he's missing?" the theatre manager inquired. "This is the hottest show in town. The touts are selling tickets on the streets for hundreds of pounds."

"I know," the woman replied. "I'm so looking forward to it. I bought my ticket five months ago and I can't wait for the show to start."

The manager suddenly thought that perhaps the woman and her husband had split up and so maybe he shouldn't pursue this line any further.

"But what about your friends," he said, still clearly in shock. "Didn't any of your friends want to come with you?"

"No they couldn't," the woman replied, "they're all at my husband's funeral!"

So a hot ticket is always a hot ticket but the hot tickets can never be created by the business.

The important point to remember in all of this is that there is one thing you (Wire Crates) and your promoter and your record company can never buy and that's the buzz. When there is a buzz around on an artist, really there is little need for promotion. You just put the tickets or CDs on sale and the buzz does the rest. The buzz is as effective as my father is with his magic match when he's lighting his fire. You can make a great record and you can do all the things you're meant to do with it and your record just may, or may not, sell. But if there is a buzz on your record just sit back and get ready to feel that heat.

The buzz usually happens at the beginning of your career and that is because newness if one of the vital ingredients for the buzz. Although that is not always necessarily the case. Take, for instance, Paul Simon and *Graceland*. Really there was no apparent logical reason why that album happened the way it did. Mr Simon was coming off the back of an album *One Trick Pony* which hadn't done very well sales-wise. But even before *Graceland* was released there was a buzz on it. The buzz happens when people start to talk about an artist or a particular album of an artist. The buzz is effective because the people talking the album up are not the people who are working on the album. The people I am referring to are agents, managers, promoters, radio producers, television producers, journalists, DJs and generally music fans who work within the music business community. All of the above people (and more) were buzzing about how special *Graceland* was, saying that it would do incredibly well and it did. It was the same thing with Dylan's last album. This was Dylan's 44th album, so how are you meant to know if it was a better or worse album than album number 29? And who even cares about that anyway? Bob Dylan released an album called *Time Out Of Mind*. It was so good it caused a buzz, sold two million copies and won him three Grammies. Mind you, I think they'll be discussing Dylan in a hundred years time, the same way they discuss Dickens and Shakespeare today. You just see if I'm not correct on that one.

At the time I am writing this, the buzz is currently on Ryan Adams, an artist Paul Fenn, my partner in Asgard, is agent for. Mr Adams makes music that connects with people the first time they hear it. He is well on his way to winning his audience.

I suppose the point in discussing this audience thing is just in a way to warn you what may or may not happen to you and to your career. There is a chance that you could make an absolutely amazing album and all of your circle of family, friends and business associates will agree with you on just how excellent it is and then you'll release it and it may do nothing. And that's not anyone's fault. It just means that your music didn't strike a chord of sympathy with the audience that we are all so interested in.

But then, on the other hand, say you make your *Blonde On Blonde* or *Astral Weeks* or *I'm Alive* or *Hats* or *Abbey Road*, who's to say that you're going to be able to successfully repeat the process? And who's to say that it's guaranteed you're going to be able to repeat it for a second, third or fourth time, or annually for several years like the record company will want and contract you to do?

I'm afraid it's not so easy to tap into something that special. It's not a coal seam you're mining. These little gems we are discussing just don't give themselves up that easy. No, it's much more difficult than that. A more likely road would be that you release your first album, the album that gains you attention you are seeking. Then your next album just might be your breakthrough album and should sell by the proverbial truckload. Then you'll have a couple of albums that will benefit directly from your breakthrough album. Then you'll have several albums of diminishing return. This downward spiral in sales will be parachuted only by your often-resisted Greatest Hits album.

And why? I don't really know. You see I'm just part of that audience we've been discussing in this chapter. For my part, it might have something to do with the fact that when I have a copy of the record *Songs From A Room* I'm happy. I can listen to it whenever I want and maybe that's all I need from that particular artist. In the music business though, we want the audience to buy every single album an artist releases and buy a ticket for every single time the artist tours. I suppose, considering the audience's other commitments and responsibilities, that's being just a wee bit unrealistic, isn't it?

The majority of artists I know and work with get it right. They produce the best work that they can do, work that they are happy with and proud to put their name onto, and the rest is down to that mythical undeterminable audience.

17. The Bright Light

"Okay. Now we know about our audience but what about our agent?" I hear you shout.

Sorry. Of course you're correct, we haven't yet discussed what the most important member of your team actually does.

Well, that's not strictly true, is it? We've already given you the secret about how to produce rain on stage – the difficult bit being to do it successfully and not electrocute everyone on stage. But of course there's more, lots more.

Okay, most people kinda know that agents are responsible for getting artists some kind of work. Those of us lucky enough to have seen DA Pennyfather's classic study of Dylan, *Don't Look Back*, have actually experienced an agent at work. I'm sorry to say that Mr Tito Burns didn't do a lot for my profession with his Terry Thomas-influenced performance in that particular film. I believe it was Tito who on one momentous occasion was overheard to say, "How do you expect me to make a living when my artists take 90% of my income?"

But apart from what Mr Burns appeared to do in *Don't Look Back*, what most of us actually do is find our artists and then find work for them in the performing arena.

An agent will represent several artists. In this instance, let's assume we are talking about a band like Wire Crates who already have some kind of a fanbase. Around the time Wire Crates are going to release their new album, they must tour to bring the album to the attention of their loyal fans. The two opposing views at this stage will be whether you should tour before the album so that you build up an anticipation for the album and subsequent sales or, if you wait until the album is out for a few weeks before you start the tour so that (a) people will be aware of your newer material and (b) the profile of the new album will have helped you sell all the tickets for your concerts. As an agent, I believe in the latter, but somehow the record companies always seem to win this particular argument by shifting the goalposts after tickets have gone on sale.

The agent will have a conversation with the artist, the manager and the record company and we will eventually agree the length of the tour, the venues, cities and countries to be covered. The agent will return to his office and contact the promoters he knows in each city on the planned tour, and will have the promoter check out the availability of the various venues. The promoters will send the availability through to the agent and the agent will then build the tour taking the availability, the routing and the artists' preferred touring schedule into consideration. Most artists have a preference for three consecutive nights of concerts, one night off, three nights back on, one off etc. It's an exact science based on strength of lungs, strength of character and anxiousness to get it all over as soon, or as late, as possible. James Taylor likes a break after every second concert; on the other hand, Mark Knopfler really hates dates off and rarely allows them to appear in his schedule. In his case I suppose it's like Loudon Wainwright the Third once sang, "If the day off doesn't get you, the bad reviewer will."

The longer the notice, the greater the availability of the venue. The greater the availability of the venue, the easier it is to build a well-routed tour. Artists appreciate tours scheduled in conjunction with a map as opposed to those put together by throwing several darts at the map in your office.

"What's a map?" Arthur asks.

Oh, I think we might have a problem here.

Perfectly routed tour under his arm, the agent then goes back to each of the promoters and advises them of the ideal night for his city. The promoter pencils the venue that night and submits a costing to the agent. The costing – as we showed earlier in the example for Hammersmith Odeon – will basically show the capacity of the venue and the ticket price. We multiply the capacity by the ticket price and we will have the gross for the concert. We divide this amount by 1.175, which gives us the total box-office take after VAT has been deducted. The costing will also incorporate lists of the costs incurred in staging the concerts. We then subtract the cost of running the show from the box-office (after VAT) figure and we have the nett amount to be split between the artist and the promoter. Usually the artists will receive a guaranteed fee against a percentage of the nett. The percentage can be as low as 75% nett to the artist, 25% to the promoter, or as high as 97.5% to the artist, 2.5% to the promoter. We're talking Rolling Stones rare air here mind you.

Once the agent and the promoter have spent a suitable amount of time haggling about how the nett should be split and what the guaranteed fee is, the gig will officially be termed as confirmed. The agent will then issue contracts. The contracts will contain all of the above plus a payment schedule – how much is paid in advance, how much is paid on the night – and the artist rider. The agent will send a copy of this contract to the manager/artist and a second copy of the contract to the promoter. Both parties will sign and return the contracts to the agent. The agent will then send the artist the promoter's signed copy of the contract and the artist's signed copy of the contract will be sent to the promoter. Phew!

With the concert fully confirmed, the promoter then officially books the venue and pays a deposit to secure the booking. He or she will then put the tickets on sale and print leaflets and posters advertising the concert – using the artist's approved artwork. He will also place and pay for adverts in the local and national press advertising the show. He and the agent will monitor the ticket sales and place additional adverts or have the artist do additional interviews as ticket sales, or a lack of them, dictate.

The agent will continue this process throughout the country, Europe or the World, depending on the stature of the artist. He will also keep his eye keenly on the artist's career and ensure that, concert-wise at least, the artist is always seen to be taking a step in the right direction. Well-paid spots on festivals with a good billing can see the artist take several steps up the proverbial ladder. A bad performance on a festival or a duet with Michael Bolton will see them slip back down several snakes.

As the agent continues with his master plan, the promoter will be attending to the business of promoting the concert and preparing for the big night. Every artist's contract that is sent out contains the artist's rider. The artist's rider is a list of requests peculiar to that particular artist. The promoter has to pay great attention to these details – the bigger the artist, the greater the attention to detail. Apparently Madonna when introduced to promoters at her concerts always informs them that they will only hear from her if she's unhappy. Artist's riders list how many stage crew (humpers – I know exactly what you're thinking, but just don't go there) will be required to help empty the artist's truck(s) and set up the gear, a process which will be reversed at the end of the night. The rider will also list: the artist's catering requirements; exact billing; the number of guest tickets they'll require; parking requirements; security requirements; hotel accommodation; and internal transportation requirements if some are included as part of the deal. Then, on the night, the promoter and his staff will stage and run the concert and deal with the artist mostly through the road crew and tour manager. At the end of the night he'll settle up with the artist's tour manager or road accountant, depending on the stature of the act, and pay over the balance of the fee plus any percentage.

The agent doesn't need to attend each concert but the promoter really should. If they can't, then they will have a representative (known affectionately as the promoter's rep) deal will all of his responsibilities. The agent will turn up from time to time, in times of trouble or glory. The agent will liaise with all of the people involved with the artist and, in instances where neither a manager nor a record company have been appointed, the agent will help to make the connection and generally vibe up the necessary parties. In the early days, baby agents were called bookers but now everyone seems to be an agent.

So where do agents come from? Or how do you become an agent? Assuming of course you want to be an agent. First off you learn how to frolic around on the beach with a half-naked – actually make that a three-quarter naked – Ursula Undress then you learn how to shake, not stir, a martini... oops... Sorry, that's the other type of agent isn't it? Well I've already described to you how I started and that's certainly one way. In the 1970s and the 1980s the majority of the London agencies filled their vacant spots with ex-Student Union social secretaries. Some of the more ambitious social secretaries saw agencies as being their short cut into the glamorous music business and have in fact now progressed into the higher echelons of the industry.

But that was then. That well-worn path is now completely exploited. Nowadays the best way for an agent to start, I would say, would be to go out and find your own act and work your whatsits off building them to the extent people in the industry are paying attention to them and, consequently, you. Another route would be to start your own (little agency) and little agencies have a habit of growing into big ones when one or more of their artists breaks (i.e. becomes successful), at which point the little agency (agent) will be swallowed up by one of the larger agencies who are perhaps not quite as successful on the talent-scouting front. But you soon discover finding your own acts is always the best, and most satisfying, way.

Regrets, I've had a few, but then again (excepting Gilbert O'Sullivan and The Waterboys) too few to mention.

In short though, an agent's main job seems to me to be that of a convincer. He starts off by (hopefully) convincing an artist to work with him. He then has to convince promoters to do what they don't want to do, to take new artists they've never even heard of and gamble money on them being successful. Finally, when the pendulum has swung entirely in the opposite direction, he has to convince the successful artist, who'd be just as happy to stay at home or in the studio, to come out and do concerts that they really don't want to do.

"Okay," you say. "That all seems fine to me but how do you produce the pure white light from out of the top hat?"

Oh yes that's the other thing an agent has to be good at. He has to be good at keeping a secret or three.

18. Resource Materials

Managers

Chris O'Donnell, CMO Mgmt., Unit 32, Ransom Dock, 35/37 Park Gate Road, London SW11 4NP. Tel: 020 8228 4000

Fraser Kennedy, FK Mgmt., Dapdune Wharf, Wharf Road, Guildford, Surrey GU1 4RR. Tel: 01483 565 010

Bob Johnson, Southside Mgmt., 20 Cromwell Mews, London SW7 2JY. Tel: 020 7225 1919

Agents

Mick Griffiths, Asgard, 125 Parkway, Regents Park, London NW1 7PS. Tel: 020 7387 5090

Emma Banks, Helter Skelter, The Plaza, 535 Kings Road, London SW10 0SZ. Tel: 020 7376 8501

Steve Strange, Helter Skelter, The Plaza, 535 Kings Road, London SW10 0SZ. Tel: 020 7376 8501

Martin Horne, ITB, 3rd Floor, 27a Floral Street, London WC2E 9DQ. Tel: 020 7379 1313

Publishers

Peter Barnes, Plangent Visions, 27 Noel Street, London W1V 3RD. Tel: 020 7734 6892

Stuart Hornall, Hornall Brothers Music, The Basement, 754 Fulham Road, London SW6 5SH. Tel: 020 7736 7891

Kenny MacPherson, Warner Brothers Records, 3300 Warner Blvd, Burbank, California 91510, USA. Tel: 001 818 846 9090

Accountants

Pat Savage, OJ Kilkenny, 6 Lansdowne Mews, London W11 3BH. Tel: 020 7792 9494

JJ, Conroy Tobin, Boundary House, 3rd Floor, 91/93 Charterhouse Street, London EC1M. Tel: 020 7608 3633

Lawyers

James Ware, Davenport Lyons, 1 Old Burlington Street, London W1S 3NL. Tel: 020 7468 2600

Russell Roberts, Sheridans, 14 Red Lion Square, London WC1. Tel: 020 7404 0444

Record Companies

EMI, Chrysalis, 43 Brook Green, London W6 7EF. Tel: 020 7605 5000

Universal/Island Records, 22 St Peters Square, London W6 9NW. Tel: 020 8910 3333

Virgin, Kensal House, 553/579 Harrow Road, London W10 4RH. Tel: 020 8964 6000

Instant Karma, 36 Sackville Street, London W1X 1DB. Tel: 020 7851 0900

Warner Brothers, 28 Kensington Church Street, London W8 4EP. Tel: 020 7937 8844

BMG/Conifer, Bedford House, 69/79 Fulham High Street, London SW6 3JW. Tel: 020 7384 7500

Publicity

Richard Wootton, Richard Wootton Publicity, The Manor House, 120 Kingston Road, London SW19 1LY. Tel: 020 8542 8101

Bernard Docherty, LD Publicity, Fenton House, 55/57 Great Marlborough Street, London W1V 1DD. Tel: 020 7439 7222

Barbara Charone, MBC, Wellington Building, 28/32 Wellington Road, St Johns Wood, London NW8 9SP. Tel: 020 7483 9205

Pluggers

Judd Lander, Judd Lander Music PR, The Media Village, 1 Wildhill, Hertfordshire AL9 6EB. Tel: 01707 656812

Agents For Record Producers

JPR Productions, PO Box 4 E & F, Westpoint, 33-34 Warple Way, London W3 0R. Tel: 020 8749 8774

Promoters

Harvey Golds… Ah come on now, away with you. Of course you'd never want to speak directly to a promoter. You'd always do it through your agent, wouldn't you? Wouldn't you?

Anyway that's it. That's your lot. Except for…

Essential Reading

X Ray by Ray Davies (Viking)
David Geffin: A Biography Of New Hollywood by Tom King (Hutchinson)
Black Vinyl White Powder by Simon Napier-Bell (Ebury Press)
I Love The Sound Of Breaking Glass by Paul Charles (Do Not Press)
The Ballad Of Sean And Wilko by Paul Charles (Do Not Press)
The Hissing Of The Silent Lonely Room by Paul Charles (Do Not Press)

Essential Viewing

Almost Famous
This Is Spinal Tap

The Essential Library: Currently Available

Film Directors:

Woody Allen (2nd)	Tim Burton	Ang Lee
Jane Campion*	John Carpenter	Joel & Ethan Coen (2nd)
Jackie Chan	Steve Soderbergh	Clint Eastwood
David Cronenberg	Terry Gilliam*	Michael Mann
Alfred Hitchcock (2nd)	Krzysztof Kieslowski*	Roman Polanski
Stanley Kubrick (2nd)	Sergio Leone	Oliver Stone
David Lynch	Brian De Palma*	George Lucas
Sam Peckinpah*	Ridley Scott (2nd)	James Cameron
Orson Welles (2nd)	Billy Wilder	
Steven Spielberg	Mike Hodges	

Film Genres:

Blaxploitation Films	Bollywood	French New Wave
Horror Films	Spaghetti Westerns	Vietnam War Movies
Slasher Movies	Film Noir	German Expresionist Film
Vampire Films*	Heroic Bloodshed*	

Film Subjects:

Laurel & Hardy	Marx Brothers	Film Music
Steve McQueen*	Marilyn Monroe	The Oscars®
Filming On A Microbudget	Bruce Lee	Writing A Screenplay

TV:

Doctor Who

Literature:

Cyberpunk	Philip K Dick	The Beat Generation
Agatha Christie	Sherlock Holmes	Noir Fiction*
Terry Pratchett	Hitchhiker's Guide (2nd)	Alan Moore
William Shakespeare		

Ideas:

Conspiracy Theories	Nietzsche	UFOs
Feminism	Freud & Psychoanalysis	Bisexuality

History:

Alchemy & Alchemists	The Crusades	The Black Death
Jack The Ripper	The Rise Of New Labour	Ancient Greece
American Civil War	American Indian Wars	

Miscellaneous:

The Madchester Scene	Stock Market Essentials	Beastie Boys
How To Succeed As A Sports Agent		
How To Succeed In The Music Business		

Available at all good bookstores or send a cheque (payable to 'Oldcastle Books') to: **Pocket Essentials (Dept SMB), 18 Coleswood Rd, Harpenden, Herts, AL5 1EQ, UK**. £3.99 each (£2.99 if marked with an *) . For each book add 50p postage & packing in the UK and £1 elsewhere.